Wildlife Film-making
Looking to the Future

Edited by Piers Warren – Foreword by Neil Nightingale

Featuring contributions from many leading wildlife film professionals

Published by:

Wildeye
United Kingdom

Email: info@wildeye.co.uk
Websites: www.wildeye.co.uk/wildlifefilm-making
www.wildeye.co.uk/publishing

Copyright © Wildeye 2011
First published 2011

ISBN 978-1-905843-02-2

Many thanks to;
Roland Clare for copy-editing
Adrian Cale, Jason Peters and Laura Turner
for development advice

Contents

Foreword

Wildlife television and films are of almost universal appeal. They are enjoyed by huge numbers of people, of all ages, around the world, a reflection of the appreciation of nature that most humans seem to share. As in all areas of the media, the last decade or so has seen a revolution, a huge explosion in the ways we can access natural history, from tiny mobile phones to giant-screen films, from interactive and personal to massive shared events, with everything in between. Conventional forms like TV and radio now compete with newer experiences: video games; 3D and 4D films; immersive attractions; live events, and the almost limitless potential of the internet. The increased variety provides seemingly endless choice for audiences, which is great for some while bewildering for others. The experience for anyone wanting to find a job or start a career in natural history media is similar – an eye-popping diversity of opportunities but also a potentially baffling array of different media, jobs and companies.

If you're considering working in any kind of wildlife media this book is a brilliant guide to help navigate and understand that confusion of choice and opportunity. But it's much more than that. It provides an engaging account of the whole industry in its many forms. Even those who've spent a lifetime working in this business will discover aspects of it they were barely aware of. I certainly did.

The first-hand accounts from a range of people not only make the book an enjoyable read, but also provide a great variety of different perspectives, and even contradictory opinions, reflecting the disparate nature of the industry itself. Despite the multiple authors, common themes come through. The clearest is the deep passion most writers share for nature itself and for telling its stories. However, almost everyone's story of how they started and progressed is different. There simply is no conventional route into this business. In most cases it has taken a hell of a lot of determination, often with setbacks along the way. What shines through in almost every account is how rewarding these jobs are. Even now, after more than twenty-five years in wildlife film-making, I still can't quite believe how lucky I've been to make a living following my twin passions of storytelling and the natural world.

Telling those stories has never been more important. The world this year has just passed the point where more people inhabit towns and cities than live in the countryside – never have we as a species been more isolated from nature. For many, their only connection with the natural world is through TV, internet or other electronic media. These have a huge role to play in inspiring everyone with the wonders of nature and its importance for our own survival. As humans reduce the amount and variety of life on earth, destroy the natural environments in which wildlife thrives and alter the very biological processes of our planet – on which both nature and we depend – it's more vital than ever that the media highlight these stories in ways that move us to care. There can surely be few more fascinating, rewarding or relevant jobs than sharing the natural wonders of our planet with millions of others, informing them about the issues that face it and inspiring them to care and to act.

Neil Nightingale, Creative Director, BBC Earth

Introduction

Whether you are an aspiring wildlife film-maker or a seasoned professional, to understand the changes that have happened within the industry over the last decade, and those that lie ahead, is of crucial importance to your career and future.

In order to explore these changes we have invited nearly sixty people involved in wildlife film-making to present their personal views. They come from many different areas of the industry, different countries, and different stages of their careers. This diversity gives us the best possible chance of predicting the changes to come. The bulk of this book is made up of these many personal contributions, split into two chapters: *Future Skills*, where we learn from skilled practitioners, which is divided into nineteen different roles within the genre; and *Views from the Industry*, where we hear from a selection of others connected with the industry, from producers to festival directors to newcomers.

Twenty years ago we would have been largely talking about wildlife films on television and a very few cinema releases, but one of the major advances is the increased number of different ways in which films can reach an audience. This can mean anything from viewing a tiny screen on a phone to a massive IMAX projection. Technological developments accelerate, and the internet expands apace: we shall explore this side of things in more detail in the next chapter: *Changes in Technology*.

As the number of platforms increases so the viewers become more thinly spread and budgets become ever smaller. The challenge to attract viewers is greater than ever and will continue to get harder. Working in wildlife film-making is more competitive than it has ever been, and to be willing and able to adapt to changes is of key importance.

Since we published *Careers in Wildlife Film-making* in 2002, here at Wildeye we have welcomed one thousand students into our International School of Wildlife Film-making. Some of these have gone on to work in mainstream television and many others have found their own routes: producing films for DVD/BD (Digital Versatile Disc/Blue-ray Disc) or for the internet or other platforms. Creative thinking combined with new technologies has enabled many to make a living through involvement with wildlife images and sound. Some others have found the industry too competitive and have preferred to retain the craft as an enjoyable hobby, one they can follow with increasing quality on a smaller budget as camera technology increases and equipment prices drop.

We've tried to keep industry jargon to a minimum throughout this book, but one expression used by numerous contributors is 'blue-chip' films. These are generally high-quality, sumptuously photographed, big budget programmes or series, such as many produced by the BBC NHU (British Broadcasting Corporation Natural History Unit). They often focus on animal behaviour and rarely have presenters or a human element. The popularity of blue-chip programmes comes and goes; for some film-makers they are the ultimate goal, for others their approach has become dated. This is discussed by many of the featured professionals in this book.

Styles of programme-making constantly shift. There have been many debates about the possible death of blue-chip, or of the hands-on-animals approach, but it seems that as the number of platforms increases so the diversity of audiences for different styles does too. There will be a need for both presenter-led and presenter-less productions for the foreseeable future. The question is, which styles will be most popular on which platforms?

It is interesting to read, throughout the case studies and essays that follow, that there is disagreement and subjectivity about certain areas of the developing industry. Some love 3D for example, others think it a passing fad. Few have yet to consider the possibilities of 4D!

Debates on the future of the industry and developing technologies are highly popular at wildlife film festivals. The aim of this book is to present current viewpoints to all, including those who are unable, or cannot afford, to attend a festival.

One area of wildlife film-making that has been hotly debated for years is the (until recently, small) number of conservation-oriented films that are made and broadcast, and the proportion of conservation aspects within any wildlife film. This is discussed by many of our contributors, in some cases most passionately.

The very fact that so many of the leading lights of our industry have generously given their time and insight to contribute to this book shows us what a special industry we are in – quite unlike any other genre of film-making. Many of us started with a love of natural history and a desire to share this with others, followed by a fascination with the technology used in film-making and a drive for quality and excellence. The future, as always, is uncertain. But thanks to the experience and wisdom of the contributors to this survey, we have the best possible chance of being prepared. Here's *Looking to the Future*!

Note that this is an international book, with contributors from all over the world: you may notice that different countries spell some words in different ways – color/colour, organize/organise, program/programme, for example. We have left the spellings true to the contributors' origins.

Changes in Technology

The wildlife film-making industry, more than any other genre, has developed alongside advances in technology. Not that technology should drive our productions (though it does in some cases) but because we strive to record such extraordinary spectacles: creatures that are tiny or huge, move extremely fast or slow, or live in the deepest ocean, or can be filmed only from very far away. All these challenges cause us constantly to seize (and in many cases help develop) the latest technological innovations in the capturing of moving images and sound.

But we're not talking about developments just in filming equipment. The industry is also controlled by the formats required by broadcasters (and ultimately by the equipment used at home by the viewing public) and by all the new ways of disseminating films that bypass broadcasters: using the internet, phone applications and so on. To make successful wildlife films these days, and into the future, you really need to keep up with accelerating technological developments, carefully choosing those that help you tell the wildlife story you are creating.

At the turn of the millennium we were discussing the developments of digital video but, at the time, 16mm photographic film was still the most commonly used format for professional productions. All that has changed. Although there are a few film-makers still using 16mm equipment, their number is dwindling rapidly and the format is likely to die out altogether. The equipment has just become too expensive, heavy, and is burdened with all the associated problems of requiring rushes to be developed photographically, compared with the immediate feedback from modern digital cameras.

We may see 35mm movie film in use for some time, especially for feature films, as it is still a high-resolution format. But its days are ultimately numbered and few wildlife producers are likely to use this equipment now.

So, digital video is the way ahead for acquisition for the time being, but even within that there is a dizzying array of definitions, bit-rates, recording media and associated costs. The question 'what is broadcast quality?' is more complicated to answer than ever.

Let's start by discussing definition. One of the major changes in the last decade is the gradual move from standard definition to high definition by many viewers and video-makers. There are still many SD (Standard Definition) television sets in homes, and many SD cameras in use, but they are being rapidly replaced by HD (High Definition) televisions (flat LCD screens being by far the most popular and affordable) and HD cameras.

SD provides 625 lines per frame (actually 576 visible lines, the rest being used for other information such as sync data and captioning) with the PAL system (used in the UK and many other countries) or 525 lines per frame (480 visible lines) with the NTSC system used in the USA and parts of South America. HD provides resolutions of either 1080 or 720 lines per frame.

Increasingly broadcasters will air wildlife films only in HD now, so if you're aiming to produce films for television you really need to focus on HD. Just to make matters more complicated there are higher resolutions than HD – such as those used by the Red One camera, which can record at resolutions up to 4,096 horizontal by 2,304 vertical pixels (often called 4K). Cameras like these are set to replace 35mm film for cinema, but are also being used for some television productions.

Although in general video cameras are cheaper than their photographic film counterparts (and in some cases *far* cheaper as we shall see later) the high-end kit used for television is often still beyond the budget of the newcomer. As well as constantly being asked whether a camera is 'broadcast standard', we are increasingly coming across aspiring film-makers who are saving up for the ultimate camera that will fulfil all their needs including possible future television broadcast. This is a dangerous path to follow!

If you're starting out now, the chances are that by the time you've made a film worthy of broadcast, technical requirements will have changed and will be higher than your camera can deliver. Not only that, but if you make a programme for television in the future it is quite likely that the camera used will be hired in for the job, or lent to you by the producers. The days of television camera operators' owning their own kit are dwindling. But that doesn't mean you shouldn't own some kit yourself – more on that later.

Although HD refers to the resolution (number of pixels) there is still much variety in quality within the format. This can be governed by the size and type of chip(s) or sensor in the camera and the speed with which the footage is recorded to memory. This speed is known as the bitrate (ie the number of bits, or units of information, processed per unit of time); with digital video we are normally measuring in Mbit/s (Mega (million) bits per second). This is governed by the recording part of your camera, so if you need to increase your bitrate it is possible, with some cameras, to add on a faster recording unit rather than replacing the entire camera. The higher the bitrate, the higher the quality of the recorded image. All this is important for television production because many broadcasters have a minimum bitrate that they will accept (and this is routinely increasing at present). A number of broadcasters (such as the BBC) publish, online, their current technical requirements for broadcasting.

The upshot of all this is that whatever kit you buy or use now will be outdated rapidly. Gone are the days (of 16mm) when a movie camera would last you for many years, possibly your whole working life!

Another aspect of camera technology that has changed rapidly is the media used for storing the footage. Initially all video cameras used tape (first analogue, then digital) and many still do. But then hard drives came on to the scene, and increasingly now cameras are using solid-state technology: recording on to memory chips. This has huge advantages for the wildlife film-maker – many hours of HD footage and sound can be recorded on to small, relatively inexpensive, chips, easily carried in  the field, that can be downloaded much faster than real-time.

This brings us to a whole new area of film technology that affects all our futures – that of handling data. Understanding all the various means of storage, transfer, bitrates, file-types and the all-important aspect of backing-up important material is essential. A newcomer with a thorough grounding in these developing digital technologies will be a useful part of the team and it is possibly a new way to enter the industry. This role is known by some as DIT (Digital Imaging Technician), and it can include aspects of setting up the camera as well. We used to say the ability to carry a tripod was the first requirement: now it is to know how to back-up the bytes! (Bytes, by the way, are a sequence of bits).

The technology of recording sound has developed alongside the evolution of cameras. These days audio recorders capture to solid-state chips or internal drives and have become smaller, lighter and ever more portable and reliable. In the Post-production Sound section of the *Future Skills* chapter, Richard Crosby from Films at 59 gives a fascinating description of the development of sound technology in the studio over the last few years.

Developments in camera technology have also been seen in a number of specialized applications such as high-speed photography (to produce slow motion, or slowmo, a much used effect by wildlife film-makers). A few years ago we were still reliant on high-speed photographic film cameras, such as Photo-Sonics, which would expose hundreds of feet of film in a few seconds. This could give excellent quality results but it was not easy to use in the field – many takes could be expensive in film stock, and you still had the problem of not knowing whether the shot had worked until the film had been developed. Now we have super-high-speed digital cameras such as the Photron or Phantom models. These can record (up to) tens of thousands of frames per second, enough to slow down the fastest humming bird's wing-beat, or chameleon's darting tongue, dramatically. But these are expensive pieces of kit – some costing over £100,000 per camera – so, again, they are likely to be hired in for the job rather than owned by the film-

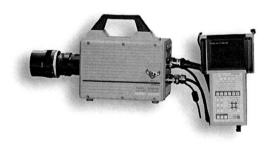

maker. The operation of equipment like this is a specialist skill, and it can be quite advantageous for an aspiring camera operator to sell him/herself as skilled in a certain area such as high-speed camera work. It's another way of standing out from the crowd.

Another example of a recent development of great use to the wildlife film-maker is the function, available on some cameras, of *pre-record* (or *pre-roll* or *post-trigger*). When the camera is in standby mode it is constantly buffering a rolling few seconds of image (buffering means loading the data into a reserved area of temporary memory (the buffer)). When you hit the record button those few seconds are committed to memory, along with everything after that point, until you stop recording. If, for example, you wanted to get a shot of a dragonfly landing on a reed stem (an action so fast that you would be most likely to miss it unless you let the camera record continually, in hope) you train the camera on the reed (where you have seen dragonflies alight before) and when one lands, press the record button. You should now have captured the whole action of the dragonfly approaching and landing. Pre-record is also available on the high-speed cameras discussed above – essential when recording unpredictable but fast events, such as a frog seizing a fly.

Alongside the development of professional cameras we have seen advances in budget cameras aimed at the amateur or semi-pro market. This has really opened up possibilities for the newcomer, who can now create quality films on a tiny budget. Although the bitrate and other aspects may not be enough to please a broadcaster, it can enable a film-maker to produce excellent material for use on DVD/BD or for the internet or other applications. It is easier and cheaper than ever to make films now – you can buy a small HD camera and a laptop with an editing program for just a few hundred pounds/dollars and do it all yourself. The process of actually making a complete film will teach you a great deal, and it is more affordable than ever. Of course this does mean that more and more people are producing films now (just see the rapid growth of YouTube as evidence) so you have to find ways to make your film stand out and reach an audience.

As well as these general-use HD camcorders we are also seeing an array of more specialist, but very affordable, cameras of great use to the wildlife film-maker. Some of these can be very small such, as nest-box cameras and action-cams (eg the GoPro series). The latter were initially designed as sports cameras – to be strapped to a cyclist's helmet, or the front of a racing kayak – but they have many other applications: for example they can be strapped to a pole and used underwater (many

come with their own waterproof housing) and, thanks to their rugged build, put in many hazardous situations where you wouldn't want to risk your main camera. They record HD to a memory card and are small, lightweight, and amazingly cheap. Of course this wouldn't be your only camera – you can't change lenses or even focus on many models, they are just point-and-shoot – but they can help you get unusual footage to make your film stand out.

We see many examples of developments for the pro market that cross over to the amateur and vice versa. One of these has been the ability to shoot video on a stills camera. Increasingly we are coming across people using a DSLR (Digital Single Lens Reflex) camera to make films in HD. And not just amateurs – they have already been used to make

productions for television and cinema too. With the large-sized sensors used in DSLRs, the quality of the picture can be superb. There are practical downsides, such as the difficulty in creating smooth zooms, but there is an ever-growing number of fixes and add-on gadgets to help. The use of DSLRs in film-making is an area we are likely to see develop far further in the near future.

So far we have been talking mainly about the technological advances in the equipment used to acquire the pictures and sound. But, as mentioned at the start, a massive change has been seen in the way audiences access the films they want to watch. The development of the internet, broadband, wireless technology, mobile phones, tablet computers and so on has made available many new routes to the audience. DVD and BD may be around for some time yet, but eventually everything with moving parts (ie not solid-state) will disappear. Memory gets ever-cheaper: increasingly we shall be surrounded by tiny, but powerful, computers – monitoring everything and feeding back to us.

We are a highly visual species and the use of moving images (luckily for the film-maker) will continue to be of great importance. There will be even more screens everywhere – from tiny ones on our wrists and phones to huge ones in our homes and on buildings. And through these screens we shall be able to access anything we want.

Inevitably the line between television broadcasts and internet streams will disappear. We shall be accessing them on the same screens. Already many teenagers spend more hours per day watching YouTube than they do watching television. It's a fast-paced attention-grabbing world and so the greatest challenge for us producers is how we shall attract our audiences – whether for a one-hour blue-chip production or a one-minute action-packed short. A number of our contributors later in this book discuss this, and the section on Multimedia Producers in the *Future Skills* chapter in particular focuses on some interesting examples.

For some this accelerating development is terrifying – for others, extremely exciting and challenging. How we find audiences for our productions, and how/if we make them pay, is still unclear – and the topic of constant discussion and speculation. Certainly there will be developments in the next ten years that we can't even imagine now. Perhaps we shall revisit the subject then, in a further book, and examine who was right, who was wrong and how the future looks for wildlife film-makers then!

Future Skills

In this section we have invited a number of skilled practitioners to talk about their careers, examine how the industry is changing, and give advice relating to their specific roles. We have chosen the categories to cover many aspects of working in the industry in much the same way as we did in the *Careers in Wildlife Film-making* book in 2002. You will see there is much crossover – some of the individuals could have been featured in several different categories – and those who make entire films single-handed pretty much fulfil every role on their own. Some people stay within one role for all of their careers, others move from one to another as they progress.

Studying other people's career-paths can offer a great insight into how the industry is changing. To reflect this, some of the case studies chosen are from people relatively new to the industry who have had to find creative ways of adapting skills and exploiting unexpected opportunities in order to get a foot on the ladder. Others have had long, award-winning careers, but one thing is clear: as the industry changes you need to change with it in order to survive. That is likely to include learning new skills and adapting your goals.

Case Studies

For each of the roles we start with a brief recap (from *Careers in Wildlife Film-making*) of the usual activities involved, and then look at one to three case studies for each. We have deliberately invited contributions from a wide variety of people currently working in the wildlife film industry, and from a variety of countries, in order to provide the widest selection of experience and views possible.

Each case study starts with the contributor's name, job description and company name (unless they are freelance). Then, in most cases, follow the names of up to three films or series that the person has worked on that are either their favourites, or productions that they are most well known for (in some cases chosen from hundreds!). This is followed by a description of what the person does, how they got started, their experience of how the industry has changed in the recent past, and their views about the further changes they expect in the next ten years or so. Finally each person offers any tips they have for others wanting to follow in their footsteps. We urge you to read all the case studies, whatever your own specialisation, to get the full picture of how the jigsaw of this industry fits together.

In the *Contributors' Index* at the back of the book you will find further information about all the people who contributed case studies to this chapter (and also those who have contributed to the chapter *Views from the Industry*). You will also find their contact details, website links etc.

The Roles:

Producer

The producer is usually in overall charge of a film project – responsible for the production within a given budget, organisation, selection of other staff, and day-to-day monitoring of progress. If the film is part of a series they may have a series producer above them, and there may also be an executive producer (who may for example also be the distributor, or managing director of the production company, who wants to keep an eye on things). But for most situations the buck stops at the producer.

The producer may well have come up with the idea for the film, may be working in a co-production with someone else who has come up with the idea (possibly the cinematographer), or may have obtained the rights to the concept. The producer will be the one who has to determine where the money is coming from for the production – a distribution and/or broadcasting contract may have already been signed, or the production may have external funding, or be funded by the producer/production company etc.

During the pre-production phase a lot of the producer's time will be spent on the telephone and computer, organising shoots and budgets, doing paperwork, and preparing for the production phase. During production the producer may accompany the film crew and oversee/direct the shoot on location, or, with a complicated multi-location production, may remain office-bound while production assistants go where the action is.

During post-production the other elements – music, narration etc – are drawn together and the producer often sits next to the picture editor to oversee this operation. The job doesn't end there as, even after the initial broadcast, time may be spent negotiating other rights, seeking further distribution/sales etc.

Caroline Brett
Producer / Director
Shake the Tree Productions Ltd.

I worked for twenty-one years for the prestigious *Survival* series making programmes around the world, including out on the ice in Arctic Canada, in the rainforests of Sierra Leone, and on a remote Vietnamese island in the South China Sea. I produced and later directed programmes for the Anglia series *Animals in Action*, *Predators* with Gaby Roslin and *Wild about Essex* presented by Tony Robinson.

More recently, as an independent director/producer/executive producer, I have made films on macaws in Peru (Granada/WNET), black caiman in Brazil (National Geographic), railway children in India (CBA, Channel 4 International) and the history of the pearl trade in Bahrain (Save our Seas Foundation). During the past three years, while I have been making marine conservation films for Save Our Seas, the foundation has won three 'Wildlife Oscars': two Pandas (Wildscreen Film Festival) and a Rocky (Jackson Hole Film Festival).

After leaving university, I journeyed through North, Central and South America. Wherever possible I visited wildlife reserves, travelled to remote regions to see wildlife, wrote articles and took photographs primarily to boost travel funds. The published pieces proved to be a great help when it came to job interviews on my return to the UK.

19

My first job was assistant co-coordinator for a consortium applying for the franchise of the first commercial radio station in Bristol. The consortium was successful and I was offered the chance to be responsible for all wildlife/animal content. At the same time, I applied to work in the *Survival* film library. I didn't get a second interview, but was asked instead if I would consider a position as a writer/producer that had just come available. I was lucky enough to be offered the job.

When *Survival* closed down in 2001 I set up Shake The Tree Productions, an independent production company, with Alan Miller, as well as working as a freelance producer/director. Now I was in a media mêlée chasing commissions with all the other 'indies'. There are no longer many guaranteed slots for wildlife on mainstream terrestrial TV. Advertising revenue is spread more thinly, which adversely affects programme budgets. Competition is intense but content/quality expectations remain high. Careers in wildlife film-making have changed. It is different now: there are new opportunities. I have recently been lucky enough to work for Save Our Seas, a marine conservation foundation. It's been a breath of fresh air to make short conservation films, work on multi-media campaigns and wildlife preservation promotional material. Charities, natural reserves, museums, zoos, societies, corporations and companies etc. are increasingly needing content for the Internet, symposiums and public displays. There's a demand for educational content for schools, video books, cable and Internet TV channels. Sponsorship is a good way of supporting the production and marketing of specialist/self-produced DVDs. Government bursaries and grants can be applied for and distribution deals negotiated. There's also the bigger picture – cinema and 3D films.

The opportunities are 'out there' and success is achievable. Determination and dedication are key qualities. Individuals need to stand out, be innovative, have their own ideas and be multi-skilled. Qualifications, work experience and attending courses and festivals: they all improve people's chances.

Go for it.

Madelaine Westwood
Producer / Director
Nutshell Productions Ltd / Great Apes Film Initiative

Invisible Photographer
Red Kite Runner
Dear Mr President

As an artist exhibiting internationally and lecturing in art colleges I was not considered to be suitable for entering the world of wildlife film-making. I had a post-graduate qualification but not in biology or zoology, so despite in-depth knowledge of animal behaviour and habitats, which had featured frequently throughout my artwork, when I tried to incorporate this expertise into the arena of film it was considered sacrilege. However my hero has always been Leonardo da Vinci – a great artist, scientist, humanist and inventor – so I believe in a world where boundaries are elastic and all that matters is the quality of the work people do, their approach to the work and what contribution this can make. But to translate this philosophy into a real-life job you need to create the conditions and opportunities where this can take place.

In my case it meant giving up a well-paid lecturing job and initially working free for six months in the best production company I could have chosen: Oxford Scientific Films. It was a glorious time of invention; OSF were instrumental in developing some of the industry's most incredible equipment, which has given us a brand-new view of the world. We used these on feature films, commercials, natural history series and interactive videos.

At OSF I learned all aspects of film-making and production, mentored by highly talented, award-winning directors, producers and cameramen. It was a privilege to be part of the team for ten years working across all the genres – from features, corporates, commercials and occasionally

21

natural history – as a camera or field assistant. However, I wanted to focus purely on natural history documentaries and my lack of biology or zoology background came back to haunt me as the policy at OSF required that personnel in NH production had to have this qualification at that time. It was back to giving up the secure life and starting again, this time on my own with the same passion for wildlife and great stories. But now I had production knowledge and a commitment to using my skills to make a difference to the many endangered species and habitats that were our 'palette'.

It hasn't been easy. As an independent I had to learn about international distribution, negotiation, co-productions, and had to build relationships with broadcasters across the world – but I would not have changed a day of it (well, maybe the odd day).

Today, Nutshell Productions produces programming for a wide range of outlets, from international broadcasters and conservation charities to local communities trying to get a message out to a wider world. The outlets may be varied but the intention is always the same: to engage a target audience, inform them, and leave them with enough knowledge to take action should they wish to.

Nutshell also believes in developing people and talent whenever it can, which results in in-house production training for newcomers (as I know just how hard it is to get into the industry) and film training for those who really need these skills to make a difference. Nutshell has expanded its UK film-making training into specific areas like conservation film-making and will be running courses not just in the UK but across the world in partnership with our NGO colleagues. This exciting development allows local communities to make their own films in their own languages with people they recognise – which is the key to starting to have change occur from within. No more white people telling them what to do: those days are gone.

I am glad to say that many of the boundaries that inhibited people entering the world of wildlife film-making have all-but disappeared. Ten years ago broadcasters believed that making conservation and issue films was a turn-off to audiences (mainly because the films we made left them upset and disempowered). Now the world has changed: with the issues of climate change, flooding, food provision, habitat loss and diminishing natural resources affecting every one of us, broadcasters have responded to this with a new wave of informative, issue-based programming. Cynics tell me that this is just a fashionable trend but I genuinely believe that we have had a sea-change and broadcasters are much more in touch with their audience. They have to be, as their audience is now scattered across so many channels – they have to keep up with what people want to see so that the revenue continues to come in. It is a hard challenge to work within: diminishing audience numbers mean diminishing sponsor- and advertising-money coming in, with the knock-on effect that we have less money to make our films while the audiences are now very sophisticated and have high expectations of quality and content.

Film-making has always risen to budgetary challenges, often by looking to technology to help out. The plethora of tiny lightweight cameras with amazing HD capability offers us the chance to explore the world anew. Seeing the intimate worlds of different species is exciting, but even more exciting is the fact that we no longer have to be intrusive. We do not have to catch animals and put them into specially constructed enclosures so we can observe their behaviour at close quarters: we can reveal the beauty, lifestyles and relationships inside animal families without affecting them adversely. Ethics has now entered the world of wildlife film-making and many of the practices that were commonplace have now been disregarded, I'm glad to say.

The new generation of cameras has allowed another major change: production teams have been reinvented, roles have become blurred and people are now multi-skilled. You don't even need to be part of a production unit as the general public can provide footage of amazing events via their mobile phone cameras. YouTube is full of great wildlife moments filmed by the general public. This new relationship between professional film-makers and the general public or local communities will only get stronger, in my view. As broadcasters become just one outlet for distributing programming, they will seek to encompass the potential for outreach programming made by the public or local communities across the world. These will bring a very personal and fascinating insight into issues that we are generally not familiar with. This will, of course, not replace the award-winning blue-chip programmes, but rather add another dimension to the available viewing schedule. It is a chance for newcomers with a passion and commitment to showcase their work for minimal outlay – the old excuses of needing expensive equipment and technical training have gone.

The world of wildlife film-making is as creative, adventurous and full of potential as ever, but I'm thankful that the hard-and-fast boundaries have dissolved. Today, entry to our industry relies on a wider range of skills: the traditional academic and research backgrounds are still valued but sit alongside creativity, research skills, attention to detail,

23

organisation, team building, invention, ability to work under pressure, tenacity, flexibility and commitment ... all values that Leonardo would approve of.

Assistant Producer

On a big film project, or a series, there is quite often an assistant producer (usually simply referred to as an AP) to whom the overall producer can delegate any number of his/her duties. The assistant producer will take some of the responsibility for ensuring the production is finished on time and under-budget – a similar role in some companies is titled Production Manager. The assistant producer may find themselves involved in any of the work described earlier for producers – basically they do whatever the producer chooses to delegate to them. This may involve accompanying the film-crew on location.

Nikki Waldron
Assistant Producer
BBC Natural History Unit

Deadly 60
Life
Life in Cold Blood

I got started in the wildlife film-making business pretty much as soon as I had finished my zoology degree, back in 2001. I spent a few months working in the bush in South Africa then started work experience at the BBC's Natural History Unit (NHU). This lasted for around a month, and led on to some (very) short contracts, mostly tape-logging and bits of research. I persevered with this somewhat hand-to-mouth existence, taking whatever work I could – including at one point having three part-time jobs, all for different productions!

In the early days my job mainly involved logging rushes (cataloguing the footage brought back from the field), which served as an invaluable introduction to the television process, as until that point my background had been only in science.

24

Some years on, I'm now a staff Assistant Producer (AP) in the NHU. In that time I've worked on a wide variety of programmes, from archive-based shows (re-packaging material from our footage library), to live output (such as *Springwatch*), and large-scale blue-chip productions (such as *Life in Cold Blood* and *Life*). Recently I have been involved in making children's wildlife programmes: *Deadly 60* and *Live 'n' Deadly*, so to explain a little about my AP role, here is a bit about those shows:

Deadly 60 is a popular CBBC series aimed at 6–12 year-olds; each fast-paced half-hour show follows our presenter Steve Backshall as he travels around the world to encounter animals to put on his 'Deadly 60' list. I produced and directed eight episodes, so was involved from the research phase right through to the edit. I would plan where to go, which animals to feature and what stunts Steve might perform, in addition to managing the logistics and all safety aspects of the shoot.

On location, my role was to direct the crew, as well as to help with the second camera filming and to take production stills. As we are a small crew everyone works together to get the content we need in a short time on location.

In contrast, *Live 'n' Deadly* is a Saturday morning CBBC show that takes the energy and enthusiasm of *Deadly 60* on the road – visiting different UK locations and broadcasting live with a cast of children, celebrities and animals! My role for this series was producing the VT inserts (short films and clips) for each show, ensuring everything was cut and packaged in time for each week's show. At the live locations I was tasked with herding the live audience of children!

The one thing I can say with confidence about the AP role within the NHU is that it is incredibly varied, and different productions will use their APs in very different ways. Some APs will be tasked with creating a sequence for a blue-chip series – involving many weeks in the field with a wildlife camera operator; equally they could be directing presenters and contributors for a fast-turnaround magazine show (like *The One Show*). A blend of skills is therefore a great asset to any aspiring AP.

Since I started in the industry there have naturally been many changes – mostly driven by the changing technology (and resulting workflow efficiencies). For example, when I first started at the BBC, if I wanted to call up a clip from a programme, I'd have to: find that clip's source on one system, then look up the tape numbers, then e-mail the library to order a VHS, then wait for them to dig out the tape, then find a VHS player to watch the tape on, then go back into the computer system and call up the master material (if I'd found what I was looking for), then head back down to collect it from the library – before finally getting that material ingested for my editor to use ...

In contrast, this year the BBC is rolling out a new system whereby you can search, access and view clips all via your desktop! Archive research will never be the same again.

Similarly, edits can now take place with those involved crowded around a single laptop, and you can shoot HD quality footage with cameras not much bigger than domestic camcorders. Is this better? Well, what I think is great is that more people can now get their hands on kit to get them started – which means those of us already 'in the business' had better watch our backs! Also, with budgets being constantly squeezed, using the right bits of kit to streamline your business means that we can still strive to do more, but with less.

Looking forward to the next ten years, I think this budget belt-tightening will continue (aside from the odd mega-production), meaning we'll all have to be clever about how we make our programmes (churning out more episodes to get an economy of scale, shoot sharing, using more archive?). We'll also need to be smart about constantly keeping up-to-date with this technology – an AP who can cut his or her own taster-tape will stand out from a crowd who can't edit – but an AP who can also back-up tapeless rushes on location and ask the right questions about processing high-speed images, or has experience of 3D filming, might have a further edge ...

However, looking at the bigger picture, the relentless march of modernisation in the way that we, as an audience, 'ingest content' (a phrase that used to include just watching TV or listening to the radio), means that outlets for films and opportunities for 'broadcast' are becoming more varied. In ten years, we'll all access the internet through our televisions – so if you post your film on YouTube, it could

26

be watched in homes just as readily as a big series on BBC1. Impressive? Scary? Exciting?

For anyone out there reading this book in the hope of stumbling across the secret to becoming a wildlife film-maker, I can only offer a few words of advice: keep smiling, keep reading, keep writing and definitely keep watching. I've never met two people with the same story about how they 'got going' – but if you really want to, you'll find a way to make films. Good luck – and I hope to meet you on the way!

Researcher

The work of a researcher can be very varied. Some researchers will spend part of their time acting as production assistants – performing any tasks needed to ensure that details of the production are ironed out. Others will be involved earlier on in the pre-production phase – helping the producer plan and write the production. This may involve researching into similar films previously produced, searching the internet for information, reading around the subject, finding out more about locations, verifying the accuracy of scientific data, tracking down experts in the subject of the film etc.

The researcher plays an important role in natural history films by finding out as much as possible about the creatures to be filmed. They will then be an important advisor to the producer as the film progresses. Some in-depth programmes may require a specialist researcher – a marine zoology expert for example.

Claire Thompson
Researcher
BBC Natural History Unit

Andy's Wild Adventures (BBC)
Wallace and Gromit's World of Invention (Aardman for BBC)
ITV Survival Anglia Wildlife Development · multiple productions

The role of a researcher varies from day to day and can be incredibly diverse. My role incorporates a number of tasks that can vary depending on the stage of the production. During the early production stages, when ideas are still in development, there's a lot of in-depth subject research involving phone bashing, e-mail writing and trawling the Internet, books and newspapers in the hunt for good stories. It's important to build good relationships with scientists and field researchers, who can offer you first-hand reliable information, as it's your job as a researcher to source interesting, factually-accurate stories for the producer: condensing a large volume of information into a concise, salient document, highlighting only the relevant points. Producers are busy people and it's your job to make their lives easier.

During the production stage, a researcher's role becomes more flexible and you could find yourself setting up shoots, hiring camera kit, acquiring location filming permits, conducting location recces and acting as a camera assistant, production coordinator and runner ... all at the same time! The latter stages of production see the researcher following up a trail of paperwork and fact-checking (annotating) scripts for submission to the broadcaster.

I became involved in the wildlife film-making industry after a lot of hard work, sleepless nights and buckets of determination. I did a BSc in Animal Behaviour then went on to do a Masters in gibbon conservation. I lived out in Indonesia for two years, working with orang-utans and gibbons, at which time I planned to go into academia. After returning to the UK, plans changed when I landed a job with ARKive.org – a wildlife conservation website based in Bristol. After a year there, doing voluntary work in my spare time while applying for every job I could find, I finally landed a job in production as a runner for Aardman Animations. Although this wasn't natural history specifically, the production experience was invaluable and after three weeks I progressed to a researcher role.

It's very important to note that during my time in all my full-time jobs I have had other (unpaid) jobs in my spare time: writing up film ideas into proposals; attending college evening courses; arranging lunch meetings with producers; volunteering for conservation film-making organisations and making my own short films and gaining experience with cameras, editing and sound recording. This hasn't stopped, and I don't think it ever will! As this is such a competitive industry, you really need to stay ahead of the game and constantly look for ways to improve

28

your skills and experience.

The work of a researcher is developing fast and increasingly becoming an eclectic mix of different roles. Researchers are becoming multi-tasking jack-of-all-trades, expected to be able to operate professional broadcast camera equipment, source and copyright-clear archive material, develop stories into viable filming sequences, set up shoots and a whole host of other things. At the end of the day this all boils down to budgets and costs, and if a production company can squeeze as many skills as possible out of a researcher, then they will. This multi-tasking role is increasingly becoming the norm, and as budgets become smaller your skills will have to expand to keep up with demand.

You need a few key ingredients to get into the wildlife film-making industry, and the most important element is to have determination – absolutely limitless determination. Couple that with a good knowledge of (and a real love for) natural history, and a sprinkling of patience, and you'll have the perfect recipe.

The reason why 'it's not what you know, it's whom you know' is a cliché is because it's true! Getting out there and meeting people is absolutely priceless. Attend events, wildlife film-making festivals, volunteer for charities, do college / evening / film / wildlife courses and direct your efforts towards achieving a well-rounded CV that shows that you are competent and capable, as well as knowledgeable and passionate. It makes all the difference if you can *prove* you have these qualities rather than just saying that you have them. Camera, sound and editing skills will really help you stand out, so make your own films: beg, borrow and steal (responsibly!) equipment, get creative and get out there.

Emma Fraser
Junior Researcher / Media Logger
Tigress Productions Ltd

Current production: *Croc Man* – National Geographic / Channel 5

"It seems to me that the natural world is the greatest source of excitement; the greatest source of visual beauty; the greatest source of intellectual interest. It is the greatest source of so much in life that makes life worth living." David Attenborough

Throughout my twenties, my varied career certainly contributed to my passion for the natural world that David Attenborough describes so well. This interest and drive has culminated into a varied career that has finally found me working within the research sector of the wildlife film industry.

The skills you need to be a good researcher are incredibly varied. Projects I have worked on, throughout the last few years, have involved rapidly developing an in-depth knowledge of many aspects and issues of the natural world and environmental politics; liaising with scientists in the field – whether it be on the phone, in person or via e-mail; programme development – which involves working closely with senior producers and being up-to-date with current affairs, within the environmental sector; fact clarification; idea development; proof reading; and general administration for the production. And that's just to name a few of the basics!

The wildlife film-making industry is incredibly competitive and, as you are reading this book, you may be wanting a few tips on how to improve your chances of establishing yourself in this sector. Here's how I got there.

The start of my career was spent travelling the world as a wildlife artist. I had always had an ingrained passion for every aspect of the natural world and, having qualified with an honours degree in the arts, I decided to specialise in natural history illustration. While collecting material for exhibitions, I would spend days in remote locations, drawing and setting up camp. This involved dealing with the local flora and fauna, deadly and numerous, most of which migrated towards my tent every hour of the day and night!

Having such experiences, I inevitably came into close contact with scientists in the field, and would spend time merrily drawing wildlife from the safety of their jeeps while they would be off collecting data. This ignited the passion for biological sciences and set the ball well and truly rolling. After returning to the UK I went back to university to study wildlife biology. On the practical side of things, I still had bills to pay, so I worked a day job to fund the course. I mention this because others may be in the same position, ie wanting to re-train, and they should know that it is possible with a busy and full life.

Having qualified (and still not 100% sure which route I wanted to follow, but with the definite knowledge that my passion was for research, fact-finding and narrative) I got a job as a metadata logger with the Wildlife Art Company, which was created by renowned zoologist Mark Carwardine. This combined my artistic abilities with my zoological knowledge as it involved finding and appending scientific information to the illustrations we were cataloguing.

At this point I realised that I needed to be more certain about which area of research I was most interested in, as there is a large spectrum of possibilities. To do this I embarked upon a mission to gain work experience with a number of companies. I was at the BBC Wildlife Magazine for a short time, alongside the editorial team, which resulted in having an article published in the monthly section of *Where to go wild in the UK*. I was also lucky enough to have the rare opportunity to shadow editors and producers at Radio 4 – *Saving Species* – and contribute to programme proposals for senior producers at the BBC.

On top of this I was also writing and developing my own ideas and implementing them, in this country and abroad, for radio and TV – something that continues, even in current full-time employment, as I also volunteer a few evenings a week, writing and editing a wildlife gardening website!

As I have mentioned, it is important to keep up to date with environmental issues and scientific research. My suggestion would be, on a weekly basis at least, check environmental news websites for

31

current scientific developments – nationally and internationally – and scientific journals. It is also important to understand the technical aspects of production. I had little or no experience with a camera, but to make myself more desirable as an employee I proceeded to enlist on numerous technical weekend courses, which varied from camera/kit operations to sound recording, script writing and production. All these are skills that are required when working in the industry, and showing that you have a basic knowledge of each reflects your ability to multi-task. An elementary but broad knowledge of kit, and a willingness and ability to help the crew in all areas of production, is invaluable.

I was initially working from home on a freelance basis. In retrospect I missed out on the broader experiences of production that junior positions, such as runners, provide. If you possess a broad skill-set, on an educational, personable and technical level, you will find that those skills will be noticed and utilised relatively quickly, even at runner position. It does seem important to start from the bottom and work your way up, and not just assume that you posses all the skills required to go straight in as a researcher in a production company. If you are applying for researcher positions and having no luck, look for those runner jobs. You will find that you will send out hundreds of CVs before you have any luck. But don't let that put you off: keep going!

My career path is a case study for anyone who feels that their deep passion is in this sector, but maybe feels as though they have taken the wrong path educationally, early on. I didn't start out with a media degree, but have still managed to get a foot in the door and have laid the foundations for a career within wildlife documentary development. The skills that I learnt when I was travelling throughout my twenties broadened my life-experience and gave me an invaluable platform to proceed from in my chosen career path. Age is no limit, and if you have the passion, creativity, talent and motivation for natural history film-making, then go for it!

Director

This is a vague category in that few wildlife films require a separate director (in the feature film sense of controlling crew and talent) – the wildlife camera-operator filming on location is often alone with no presenters to direct.

Occasionally the producer or assistant will be on location, and to a certain degree will direct the camera operator. They may be describing what sort of shots they are after, any special effects required, what animal behaviour is essential to the story of the film, etc.

There are exceptions, however, when directors are needed on wildlife films. In a situation where several cameras are being used, for example: the director will determine which camera operator aims to capture which footage, or angles, or activity and so on. This ensures that the producer and picture editor get the shots they need to tell the story.

Furthermore, with presenter-led programmes, a director is often needed in a more traditional sense – to direct the presenter and the cameras involved. Additional cameras are encountered more frequently in shooting a presenter – so there will be more need for a director to control the situation.

Joe Yaggi
Founder / Creative Supervisor / Director / DOP
Jungle Run Productions

BumiHijau.TV (Green Planet Television) – Indonesia-wide environmental TV network. Founder, Exec Producer
Heads Above Water – BBC World & TVE. DOP & Co-Director Indonesia
South Pacific – BBC Natural History Unit. Location Manager, Indonesia

An Expat Director's Diary

There are many ways to skin a cat – and many ways to enter the business of documentary and wildlife film. The industry is ever-evolving as appetites for programming change, media platforms advance and budgets fluctuate. And while conventional television career paths will continue to exist and indeed form the bedrock of the industry, I think there will always be room for unconventional approaches to life in this business.

I'm a film-maker, a director/DOP (director of photography), and I'm an expatriate. For me, these components of my life are inseparable. I didn't come into our industry through any normal channels. In retrospect, the groundwork for what I would become was laid at an early age – whenever National Geographic or Wild Kingdom came on, the TV was mine and woe betide anyone who tried to touch it. But the film-maker in me stayed below the surface until, in my mid-twenties, I nearly got booted from college, struck out on the road, and had an

33

epiphany, standing in front of a bullet-riddled building at Makerere University in Kampala, Uganda.

Returning to university back home, I went into anthropology and on Day 1, as a twenty-something returner surrounded by eighteen-year-olds just out of high school, I had another epiphany ... this time watching a film by the renowned ethnographic film-maker, and now personal hero, Timothy Ashe. I then found out we had an on-campus television station, but it was primarily staffed by film students. They eventually let me in, I believe in part because I simply would not go away. And as the ball started rolling, my seasonal river-guiding job evolved into a video-kayaking job and I was off ...

Whitewater video-kayaking taught me a broad range of skills, not the least of which was good shooting under harsh conditions. In this environment, if you screw up, you could drown your camera or worse, drown yourself. Everywhere I worked I also made a film – a short on an earthquake in Costa Rica, a short on a sustainable development project in Zambia. These films, combined with the work I was doing for the river companies, and heaps of personal research, taught me the foundations of documentary film language. After stints on rivers in California, Central America and Africa, I landed here in Indonesia in 1993. What I thought would be a six-month stop-over has turned into an eighteen-year journey. Through this time I've continued to learn my craft and build my skills (something you should never stop doing) and I've figured out, through a fair bit of trial and error, how to build and run a production company under some fairly unusual conditions.

My company, Jungle Run Productions, is based on the island of Bali and conveniently located right in the center of the Indonesian archipelago. Indonesia is an amazingly rich and varied country. Its

18,000 islands are steeped in biodiversity (a lot of it under threat) and harbor hundreds of cultures and languages, not to mention an amazing history. And it's been primarily within this workspace that we've come to be known for specializing in environment, natural history, education, socially-conscious film-making and media, and production support for others. It's been an exciting and humbling experience thus far.

Jungle Run is relatively small, with staff that ranges from twelve to fourteen people, mostly full-time with a few freelancers. My team is primarily Indonesian and they're all very cool. We also work with foreigners in varying capacities, usually as managers or trainers and occasionally in more traditional roles on a project basis. And my partner, Djuna Ivereigh, frequently jumps in to help with writing, web design, photography etc. My philosophy has been to try, as much as possible, to build local talent and expertise, passing on what we've learned internationally to local film-makers who work with us. Many of our staff had television and feature film experience prior to joining Jungle Run, others didn't. And for the most part, they tend to find us, not the other way around. At the end of the day, what we do here is a group effort.

Owning a production company is an all-consuming endeavor. Balancing projects and clients, budgets and people, is hard work. And if you are to succeed, you have to understand not only the entire production process, but also the nuts and bolts of running a business. Throw a foreign country and a foreign language into the mix, along with weird government regulations and often massive cultural differences, and you're in for a wild ride.

Finding the footing for relative success has been as much about understanding and coming to terms with where we are and how to function in the region, as about figuring out how to parlay our experiences and location into an industry presence.

Here are a few things I've learned in the process:

- You've got to be flexible. Things will not always work out as planned
- You've got to focus on quality in everything you do
- You have to consistently promote yourself and your company
- You need to be pro-active in learning, keeping up with changes, and engaging the industry
- You need patience and compassion
- And it helps to have a sense of humor
- You need to be culturally sensitive and aware of cultural differences
- You need to take care of the people around you

- And in order to ensure a long-term support and continued success, you need to be willing to share experiences and create opportunities for others

I'm listed here as a director and DOP, which I am. But the real story is more complicated. In Jungle Run nobody has just one job – we all multi-task. Most small businesses are like that, of course, but it runs counter to the way conventional television careers are structured. I believe that flexibility and adaptability have helped keep Jungle Run going through two economic meltdowns, five presidents, a series of major bombs and a string of natural disasters that led to the failure of countless businesses, production companies included. And I think another reason we've been able to do this is because we stick with what we love and we've created a niche.

In order to stay viable, Jungle Run usually has multiple tracks of work going at any one time. We're involved in about 15–25+ hours of production each year. And as it can get quite hectic, we break it down loosely into five departments:

In-house production
This covers projects where we are responsible for everything from concept to completion and includes at least half of our total production workflow in any given year. These projects require the most man-hours and resources and are often the most satisfying. Here are a few examples:

- For broadcast projects we work with a range of people: BBC, National Geographic, Al Jazeera etc. For instance a few years back we produced a film, chronicling a twenty-three-day transect of Borneo by rivers that won at a festival in California. This appeared in part on ABC News in the States and was aired on Nat Geo's former A1 channel as part of a series called *Game For It*. For Al Jazeera we produced a film on breast-feeding and infant formula marketing for their *People and Power* strand. And after the Asian tsunami, we produced twenty shorts following two young girls from Aceh as they, their families and communities, struggled to recover from that disaster and rebuild their lives over the course of a year. These shorts were broadcast around the world.

- On the educational non-broadcast front, we recently completed twenty hours of agricultural-focused training films for USAID that were shown all across the country to hundreds of thousands of people, from tiny villages to schools to local TV stations.
- We also produce environmental, cultural, and corporate films for museums and organizations like WWF, TNC and Greenpeace. This year, for example, we're producing monthly forest reports for WWF's Year of Forests campaign, and a museum installation film for Australia.
- And finally we're actively writing and pitching broadcast stories, and produce our own personal projects. As I write, we're producing a series of PSAs, bumpers and stings for an environmental television network we're launching. But more on that later. (PSAs are public service announcements, bumpers are transition segment used in broadcasting, stings are short sequences used in films and TV as a form of punctuation).

Securing projects like these takes time and effort and a few good breaks. I attend film festivals and pitch-sessions whenever funds allow and spend a significant amount of time networking. I also place Jungle Run on production lists, participate in professional organizations and stay active in social media. This also helps with the next department in Jungle Run:

Location and Production Management and Film Permits
These projects, twenty major ones to date, are a significant part of our business. They have required establishing strong contacts in the government, and professional contacts across the country and across a range of industries. These projects are all about logistics, access, and helping other producers and broadcasters achieve their goals regardless of where they want to shoot. And we break the work down like this:

- Location and story research
- Film permits, customs and immigration
- On-site location and production management
- Troubleshooting

These projects can get quite complicated. Two significant ones that come to mind include:

- A project with MTV that required shooting in thirty locations across seven islands in two weeks. Set-up took four months and we had to charter our own 'plane to pull it off. This was our first major location management project and, because it was so complicated, it made many of the projects that followed much easier, except:
- *Man versus Wild* on the island of Sumatra for Discovery. For this two-week shoot, we spent six months in prep and recce'd on the ground for eight weeks. My immediate staff was eighteen people and we employed over three hundred people in total including all the canoe jockeys, cooks and porters.

These projects can also be great fun; here are two more brief examples:

- *South Pacific*, BBC Natural History Unit. For this project we trekked into the highlands of Papua to an area where, literally, no outsider had ever been, to shoot the elusive Dingiso Tree Kangaroo. This also took months of prep, primarily convincing the government and mining industries in the region that we were coming only to film wildlife (it's a highly charged and politically sensitive area) but it was one of those trips that changes your life.
- *Last Chance to See*. In the Indonesia episode we explored Komodo National park with Mark Carwardine and Stephen Fry. Having been a huge Douglas Adams fan, it was great to work with Mark and Stephen and the crew as they re-lived the journey that led to Douglas and Mark's original book, also called *Last Chance to See*.

Crewing
For these jobs we're hired guns, from directors to camera operators and from sound recordists to translators. We've worked with major broadcasters, production companies and NGOs from around the world as crew. For these projects we need to be fast and nimble, often moving on short notice. They're great work and very good at keeping our skills sharp.

Stock Footage
If you've got quality stock, it can be a good source of passive income. Preparing your footage for stock is key and I think it's better to do it in-house, rather than having an agency do it and charge you accordingly. Initially it's a time-consuming job but the additional income certainly helps pay the bills.

Green TV Network
Of all the interesting projects we're involved in, this is my personal favorite. Some years ago we developed a relationship with TVE, the producers of *Earth Report* for BBC World. Jungle Run became their

production and distribution partner in Indonesia. Initially we were distributing their films to NGOs, schools, and taking them to conferences such as Earth Day, social/environment forums etc. We also produce and crew with TVE when *Earth Report* productions take place here.

A few years ago the Indonesian government passed new laws encouraging the development of local TV stations. Seeing an opening to expand the audience, we began contacting these stations and offering our programs, which we adapted for Indonesian viewers. We've now partnered with fifty local TV stations that beam our programs into homes across the country, in effect creating the first TV network in the country focused on environment and socially-angled television programs. At about 240 million people Indonesia has the fourth-largest population in the world, and the provinces and cities where our local partner stations live represent about 75% of that. As these kinds of programs are new for audiences here, and the country has been experiencing such rapid change, we're hoping to have a positive impact on the social/environmental debate.

Recap

While I never intended to stay in Indonesia, the country got a grip on me in the early 90s and hasn't let go. During this time, I've adapted and evolved with the changes here in the region and so has Jungle Run. Working overseas is rife with challenges. But at the same time, I'm a firm believer that placing oneself outside the box, and just on the edge of the mainstream, can open doors to unique and special opportunities. While having some formal television experience could be beneficial in creating a production company of your own, I'll be the first to say that it certainly isn't necessary. It's about innovation, adaptation and persistence. I think if you stay focused on the sides of the industry you love, build solid skills and contacts, stay inquisitive and accept nothing less than the best of yourself, you can create a viable career, production company, and lifestyle, anywhere in the world you want to be.

Rita Banerji
Director / Cameraperson
Dusty Foot Productions

The Wild Meat Trail (Panda Winner Wildscreen 2010)
Shores of Silence (Panda Winner Wildscreen 2000)
The Last Migration (Panda Winner Wildscreen 1994)

It was February 2009. We had just finished shooting for the day in a remote forest in Meghalaya in north-east India. We shared a meal with one of the families in the village and started walking back to our vehicle, parked a few kilometers away across the paddy fields. It was a starry night, but was otherwise pitch-dark everywhere. As we neared the paddy-field, we were struck by an amazing sight: a sea of fireflies against the dark landscape. They were like free stars floating in the fields, merging into the starlit sky. And all around us the sound of the night-frogs and crickets.

This was after more than fifteen years in the field and I think these are the moments that define one's journey as a wildlife film-maker. I feel blessed for being able to choose to follow my heart. If anyone asks me what you have to do to become a wildlife film-maker, I would still say that, if it is something that you really want to do, you just have to persist and the doors will open up.

Just out of college, I worked on wildlife films for ten years before striking out on my own. In 2002, I started Dusty Foot Productions with Shilpi Sharma, a colleague and friend.

At that time, the Wildlife Trust of India (WTI), along with the Arunachal Pradesh Forest Department, was releasing captive bear cubs into the wild for the first time. The cubs had lost their mother to hunting and had been hand-raised at a rescue centre. WTI had no objections to our documenting the story as long as we did it under our own steam. We did not have funds but were determined to follow the cubs' journey into the wild.

40

Wildlife and environment films have the potential to transform: a strong tool to explore issues, generate thought and create dialogue. I was driven by the need to find the truth, including the question of hunting and whether it was sustainable. For the story to reveal itself powerfully it was essential for us to spend time out in the forests tracking the bears and the people who lived around them.

It was also important to think about financing the project. As independent film-makers the ability to move fluidly between direction, production and fundraising is essential.

Creativity is not limited just to telling the story, but is equally a requirement to make it come alive as a viable film. How do you design a project so the idea survives; raising funds through regular channels; through non-traditional ways; by gathering logistical support; through collaborations? It is about working out the options and details at every step. This constant search helped us put together the necessary finances for our project. Of course it helped that we were both camera-people.

While the bear story evolved I was constantly looking out for other assignments. In the early days we took on projects even if they were low-budget. It helped us explore. We did films for as little as US $1,800, but made possible with perks such as waivers of wildlife park fees, access to logistical support and networking. Within a year we began to be known as Dusty Foot Productions.

In the midst of other projects we ensured that we consistently went back to track the bear story. With time we realised that it required a much deeper understanding of hunting within the context of indigenous communities, and their traditional link with the forest and animals. Patience, openness and understanding were key to getting it right. These aspects have remained fundamental to most of our other projects.

41

Getting around was rough: long treks across forested hills; sleeping bags and tents; rickety buses for long-distance runs; jeeps stuck in rain-fed rivers and, in most places, no electricity! Fortunately the introduction of affordable broadcast level cameras and formats like DVCAM made it all possible for us. Smaller cameras and long-lasting batteries saw us through, and enabled us to get some unusual gritty sequences.

Our strongest partnerships have been with non-profit organisations in India who work with wildlife, environment and communities. Here everything is connected: animals, plants, people and their livelihoods. A wildlife film needs to integrate all these aspects of the core theme – conservation and sustainability.

This focus strengthened our work and helped expand our portfolio of projects. The more we did, the more we were approached by new groups and individuals. While there were no big budgets, the sheer number of film projects made it feasible for us.

We finally got funding for *The Wild Meat Trail*, an offshoot of the bear project, in 2008. It took us six long years. But the process that led to this laid the foundation for our work. The trailer was seen by one of our friends from Keystone Foundation, who suggested that we submit it for an IUCN grant. We were selected.

The funding helped us focus on post-production. We went through several versions of the script and edit until we were happy with it. *The Wild Meat Trail* went on to win a Panda Award at the Wildscreen Festival 2010, in Bristol, UK.

The funding also helped start our outreach work: 'Under the Canopy'. This is a specialised wildlife education programme that trains teachers, working in villages, as well as public schools in the north-east region. This aspect, added to the films, has opened up avenues for more support through grants that combine films with an education – awareness outreach.

Currently we are working on *The Turtle Diaries*, under a grant from Save Our Seas Foundation, with a similar emphasis on film and outreach. We are also in the process of setting up a video documentation centre on wildlife and environment in the north-east of India.

The first bear project, which we decided to be persistent with, opened many doors over the years – in terms of understanding, perspective, engagement, other wildlife films, shooting assignments, and the building of a network and credibility.

To summarise; a career in wildlife film-making requires a conscious commitment to the goal, flexibility and light-footedness, preparedness for change and restructuring, acceptance of rejection, patience and persistence! Soon the pieces of the jigsaw start coming together and a path emerges. We are still learning ...

Self-Shooting Producer / Director

This is an increasingly common description for the independent camera operator who works often on their own, is likely to have come up with the idea for the project, and is in overall control of operations in the field. In many cases this can be seen as a combination of producer and camera operator roles – the self-shooter is also likely to be in charge of funding, sales etc. That isn't to say it's necessarily a one-person-band outfit; it is usual for other experts to be involved, especially in the post-production phase, such as narrators, music composers and so on.

Patrick Rouxel
Cameraman / Director
Freelance

Alma
Green
Tears of Wood

Since 2003 I have dedicated my time and money to making films aimed at raising awareness about deforestation, loss of biodiversity and bad animal treatment. I do this independently, free of all political or commercial interest. My films are driven by empathy: they are my way of helping the forest, the wildlife and all the victims who don't have a voice to protest or defend themselves. My films are a citizen act for a better world.

I decided at the age of thirty-six to make films for conservation as a result of a midlife crisis. After more than ten years working in the production of digital special effects for commercials and feature films, I bought myself a camera (a Sony PD100) and went to Indonesia for three months on a tourist visa for my very first filming experience. Once back home, I learnt how to use Final Cut Pro and edited my first film, *Tears of Wood*.

I continued working part-time as a digital special effects supervisor – so as to make some money – and soon went back to Indonesia to make my second film, *Losing Tomorrow*. My problem was that my films were not reaching a wide audience because TV broadcasters showed no interest in them. So I decided to make my third self-produced film, *Green*, available for free download on the internet and make it copyright-free for any public screening. Luckily, the film has received more than thirty awards in festivals worldwide; it has been broadcast on ten TV channels; it is downloaded every day from around the world, and is presently being used as an educational tool by NGOs, schools and universities. *Green* proved to me that a homemade conservation film is able reach a wide audience through free download on the web. My

44

latest film *Alma*, also self-produced and copyright-free, is equally available on the net. I hope it too will reach a wide audience.

I finance the making of my films through different means: by selling my raw footage to NGOs or production companies, by selling my finished films to TV channels, by inviting people to make donations on the films' websites, by working as cameraman or director for environmental NGOs and by giving talks in schools and workshops. I live simply, with as few expenses as possible, and invest most of my income into my films. When shooting, I travel alone or with a friend for the sound recording: I carry only a small camera (Canon HXA1) and a tripod. I then edit on my laptop and have friends to help me with key steps in post-production such as sound design, Foleys, colour-grading, graphics, music and mix. Luckily, making films 'for a good cause', without commercial interest, draws many professionals to help me at no cost.

I have managed to make a niche for myself in the wildlife-conservation film industry thanks to the fact that in the last ten years the price of high-quality cameras and editing equipment has gone down, while the internet flow has gone up. With this trend continuing, it will be increasingly easy for others to follow my footsteps. The good thing about working the way I do is the creative freedom that comes with it. Having no producer or broadcaster allows one to break away from the formatted documentaries one sees on TV. The counter-side is the hardship of doing it all by yourself, always working alone to get the films done. On a more personal note, what I find most difficult in my work is witnessing so much suffering around the world. I get very depressed at seeing what mankind is capable of, and find it more and more difficult to find the energy to film these horrors.

Download *Green* from www.greenthefilm.com
Download *Alma* from www.almathefilm.com

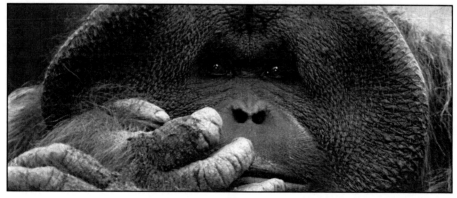

Adrian Cale
Self-Shooting Producer / Director
Freelance

Tarsier Towers – Channel 5
Panorama: Palm Oil – Dying for a Biscuit – BBC
Gibbons: Back in the Swing – Animal Planet / Discovery Networks

I work in the wildlife film-making industry as a self-shooting producer/director: both on a freelance basis for independent production companies, and through my own projects produced under the moniker of Pupfish Productions.

This allows me to develop my own programme ideas and bring them to market or work as part of a crew where ideas – and problems – are shared, but where the daily stress of managing a production falls into somebody else's lap!

For my own projects I research and develop them from the ground up. Once researched, the idea is written up into a treatment or pitch-document and the programme story, main characters, budgets and required kit etc are expanded upon. There are meetings with commissioners and production executives and if you are lucky – really lucky – someone somewhere likes the proposal and you are away.

But this is only the beginning. You now have to shoot the programme, work with sound engineers, musicians and editors, write scripts and tightly hold the hand of your commodity through the post-production process and beyond. There are then further deals to consider, with territory rights around the world: but that is for another day. Alternatively, a production company will have gone through the whole pre-production process before picking up the 'phone to speak to me. The role is then very different and often very varied, depending on what skills and responsibility I am being asked to bring to the table.

In a sense I have the best of both worlds.

I tend to think of this as a trusted role where clients rely on me to think on their behalf in the field, organising people, juggling budgets and ensuring the story is there, while at the same time creatively thinking for myself, shooting the film footage that will be the very essence of any story idea. Knowing what the executive producer or commissioner wants is just as important as knowing what your editor will need in terms of sequences when the project gets back and enters post-production. It needs a divided brain: one half thinking wholly in terms of the production, the other thinking only in creative and technical terms through the eye of a camera.

What does the audience expect to see? What do I like to see when I watch television? Is this picture aesthetically pleasing or is there a better angle or setting?

Yes, it can be stressful – but I wouldn't have it any other way.

My route to wildlife film-making was a somewhat unorthodox one, and one which I began later than most in my professional life.

Natural history has been a constant interest in my life ever since I can remember. As a youngster I filled the family home with aquaria and cages, keeping and breeding all manner of furred, feathered and finned fauna. Others read *The Beano* while I read *Animals Magazine* (the precursor to *BBC Wildlife Magazine*). I sat in front of the television engrossed in wildlife programmes, and often recorded favourites on old VHS cassettes for viewing over and over again. I joined all manner of clubs and societies and would visit zoo collections around the country as a member of the Zoological Society of London's Young Zoologists' Club. I was, and still am, a wildlife geek!

But I also loved writing and the performing arts, both of which featured heavily in my life before I took the plunge into wildlife film-making. A few roles in the then-fledgling computer-gaming industry saw my press-release and copywriting skills move me into a marketing and corporate life. This didn't resonate with me as much as the one day a week I was giving up to volunteer as a keeper at London Zoo. So as the aviaries in the garden increased and the burgeoning aquariums bubbled in the house, I changed tack. I decided to combine my creative life with my love of natural history and become a wildlife film-maker.

I taught myself how to use a camera and, after attending various film-making short courses, took the plunge. I had been pondering over a programme idea for some time and decided just to make it, quite literally. Sitting alone in Africa with a camera, an idea, and no broadcast or production partner was unconventional and probably unwise. On my return I managed to find an editor and musician who volunteered to help. We would all get paid if the project got off the ground. One year later the project still hadn't got off the ground. I was much poorer but much wiser and certainly in a position to move forward. This industry is very giving, and, encouraged by the feedback from various wildlife film-making luminaries, I managed to get the film a distribution deal. It was never shown in the UK but was, I am assured, big in Gibraltar, Eastern Europe, Spain and Portugal. The little revenue the film did recoup was quickly invested in the next project. I was up and running.

What I did then, I probably couldn't do now. In the last ten years the industry has changed dramatically. It used to be so much easier with Standard Definition where the format was universally accepted by all broadcasters. But the arrival of High Definition has brought wildlife programming to life in spectacular fashion, and with it, a whole load of broadcast restrictions have arisen. Certain cameras are OK for some channels and others are not. Approved bitrates and camera chip-sizes have been changing all the time, and it is now very risky as an independent to buy a camera meeting today's broadcast spec and expect to get three productions'-worth of investment out of it before the specs change again. On the plus side, however, is the programming: wildlife films jump out of the screen and grab your attention like never before. The detail is simply jaw-dropping and fantastic to watch.

The number of viewing options has increased and the audience has diversified. There are so many more channels now where you can find natural history programmes in all manner of styles. But with more choice comes the risk of smaller viewing figures as the audience spreads out. Online viewing and interactive websites are offering us more and more choice and that's a great thing. We have a lot of options and vehicles by which to showcase our films, and that provides us with the next challenge, which is how to keep everybody happy at the same time. As film-makers, it is essential that we constantly upgrade our skill-sets to accommodate the emergence of new technology as well as the emergence of these new audiences.

There will be further changes and, no doubt, further broadcast revolutions, but one thing is sure – people love watching wildlife films. The very number produced each year is testament to that, and being lucky enough to make them is just as exciting today as it was when I started.

What advice would I give to anyone starting out today?

If you want to get rich it is the wrong profession for you. Do the networking and try and build up that contact base. If you have a genuine passion for communicating the wonders of the natural world, and are determined to do so, there is no reason why you will not succeed. Patience and humility will open doors eventually – persevere and stay positive.

Dean Burman
Film-maker / Cameraman / H.S.E Media Diver
Waterwolf Productions

Nature of Britain – BBC1: Scientific advisor/ supplied footage
The One Show – BBC1: 2nd underwater cameraman/contributor
The Canals of England – NHK Europe: Cameraman/advisor

I am a wildlife film-maker and freelance cameraman. I have recently finished working on a film for the Japanese broadcast channel NHK Europe, entitled *The Canals of England*, on which I was hired as a freelance shooter and advisor using HDCAM and HDV for topside, and Polecam for the underwater sequences. I am actively building up a stock library and also enjoy making short films for my website: in these I also try a bit of presenting. My journey into film-making started in 2002 while on a scuba-diving holiday to Micronesia in the Western Pacific. After hiring a housing for my video camera and editing some short 'holiday'-style films, I was told by two friends who were, luckily for me, prominent natural history cameramen, that I had 'an eye' for camera work: they recommended I should pursue a career in the industry.

I have always been a very passionate enthusiast for wildlife and wildlife programmes but thought that these amazing jobs were for the chosen

49

few and out of my reach. Yet their kind words gave me the inspiration at least to try and give it a go. To gain some experience I attended a Wildeye course and got to help out a friend – leading time-lapse cameraman Tim Shepherd – on shoots, including one set for the blue-chip series *Planet Earth*. Finding actual work experience was, and still is, very hard, so I decided to make my own films and gain some experience.

My first decision was to enter my films into festivals, both local and international, just to get my work out there. My first two films *Um El Faroud, From Tragedy to Tourism*, about an oil-tanker turned artificial reef, and *Lair of the WaterWolf*, about the private life of the notorious freshwater fish the pike, were well received and won numerous awards. Both these films were totally self-funded and were a real labour of love. I think this really proved my commitment and passion for my art.

From my perspective the main change in the industry is that nearly everyone has better access to good quality cameras and equipment. HD cameras are readily available, and getting cheaper, as is decent editing software. It is more cost- effective for companies to source good quality stock footage, or hire camera people closer to the subject, rather than send out crews to distant locations. Then there is the constant rise in the number of Media Studies students and people wanting the dream ticket: as crews are increasingly featured as the stars of the show there will undeniably be more entrants to the industry who are looking just for fame.

The positive side is the growth of avenues such as satellite channels and the internet. There have never been so many potential clients.

Budgets will not be of terrestrial TV standards, however. The future does looks brighter for smaller, independent shooters, and film-makers who want to get their work shown. I am in awe of technology: HD, 3D, what is next? Bring on the holodeck, like in *Star Trek*, and then we shall be able to visit all those beautiful places without leaving the comfort of our front rooms.

For newcomers to the wildlife film-making industry the future, I think, is both exciting and daunting. I get asked all the time 'How do I get into the industry?' Well am I actually *in* the industry? I have what I like to call a 'day job' which helps fund my own personal shoots, and I know of many people in my situation who have been trying to get 'into' the industry for years. The BBC NHU is for many of us the holy grail of wildlife film-making, and working for them is always going to be a dream job, but there are plenty of other production companies and broadcasters out there.

Some snippets of advice I can give are to keep at it, get out there and film, enter film festivals, make a show-reel and send it to everyone, try and copy the top shooters' techniques you see on television, take a wildlife filming course, and try not to worry about having the latest and greatest equipment as it will be upgraded before you know it! Get as much knowledge about the natural world as you can ... did I say get out there and film? The biggest leg-up you can ever have is to have family or a friend in the industry, but if you're not that lucky, get yourself to festivals, join forums and *network*! Finally, to all of you starting out and those of you already 'there', good luck in all you do ... I hope to see you in the field.

Cinematographer/Camera Operator

The camera operators are the people who physically operate cameras in the field. A 'lighting cameraman/woman' or 'director of photography' is a senior camera specialist who will decide how the camera operator(s) will work in terms of lighting/lenses/angles etc. In some cases this position is also called 'cinematographer'. In wildlife film-making, however, it is unusual to have a separate lighting cameraman/woman – usually there is either just the one camera operator or, if several, one of them will take the lead role.

These days camera operators need to have a thorough understanding not only of photographic techniques, but also of all the computer-technology connected with storing and transferring video files, backing

51

up footage and so on. As camera-technology becomes increasingly complex and sophisticated some camera operators choose to specialise: high speed camera-work or 3D productions, for example.

Gavin Thurston
Cameraman / Director / Presenter
Freelance

Human Planet
Life
Planet Earth

I have been in this industry since I left school and I am currently still a wildlife cameraman, though I also film presenter-led programmes, straight documentaries, commercials, corporates, festivals etc.

I took my first photograph at age nine, of an orca at Windsor Safari Park, and that sparked two passions – photography and wildlife. The day I left school I knocked on the door of Oxford Scientific Films (OSF) with my photographic portfolio and was offered a holiday job, for no pay, until I went to university. Despite only getting 'bus fare and lunch I had found what I wanted to do. I skipped university and managed to get a full-time job at OSF, a kind of apprenticeship. I cut my teeth in the industry making tea and sweeping floors while watching and learning from the then masters of the industry. I gained experience working in the slide library, building studio sets, helping out on feature films and commercials – but mostly enjoyed being part of the wildlife film-making there. However, with a sought-after job comes rather low pay and I found I had to get evening work to make ends meet.

Slowly, though, over the years I learnt valuable information that would further my career, and was trusted to get more hands-on with cameras.

After four years at OSF I felt I needed wider experience (and a pay rise) so I started applying for work elsewhere in the industry. After several failed interviews I secured a job as assistant macro cameraman for the BBC in Bristol. There I made more tea, swept more floors but also got to learn more from a different set of talented professionals. Also, importantly, I started to get my first assistant and camera credits, the all-important CV credibility factor.

In 1989, still struggling financially and feeling my ambitions were being held back by the slow wheels of the big corporation, I took the plunge and went freelance as a cameraman. Working on average 240 days a year, I forged experience and reputation. For a fuller list of programmes I've contributed to, see my CV page at www.gavinthurston.com. Amazingly I am still self-employed, doing mostly what I love.

The media industry is constantly evolving and I am not sure that there has been any more change in the last ten years than in the ten years before that. To stay employed means being able to adapt and change, keep up with technology and style; Sir David Attenborough is the master of that.

One of the biggest changes I have seen is the final swap from film to digital. Initially I resisted the change: not to be stubborn, but because early on the quality of digital didn't yet match the 'old' film. Now, though, I would say that digital has evolved to equal film, and beats it in terms of ease of use. At the flick of a switch I can now change the camera sensitivity, I can slot in five memory cards and record six hours of footage without stopping (God forbid). The cameras have 'pre-roll', recording all the time to RAM, so when you push 'record' you can actually save to memory something that happened ten seconds before, meaning in theory you'll never miss a shot. Also with film you couldn't watch the shots back to check them: now you can be sure you have all the shots in a sequence before you head home.

I imagine that in the next ten years we are going to experience some real technological innovation. Now that cameras are effectively elaborate computers, the exponential rate of change in computing power and data rates will mean we shall have the ability to record more information: better colour-depth, less compression of the pictures, higher resolution. Cameras will have even better tonal and contrast range and the ability to record higher frame rates (slower motion).

Composite construction will, I hope, reduce the weight of kit we have to carry too. We already have carbon-fibre tripod legs: bring on the lightening revolution and help us reduce the sheer weight of kit we cart around the globe!

Also in the next ten years I think that conventional broadcasting will diminish and more quality content will be internet-based with pay-per-view, subscriptions and on-demand programmes available. The one thing of which I am sure is that there will always be an appetite for wildlife films and that science will continue to discover new species and behaviours for us to film.

I would say that nowadays it is easier to create an impressive portfolio to try and get noticed. In my early days each photo would cost pounds to process and print; today a DVD costs less than one pound to produce and can contain photos, video, CV, interactive PDF, sound, music, and so on – a chance to showcase your multi-media skills as well as your camerawork. High quality digital cameras are more accessible but even with a low-end DSLR you can compete with the pros. If you have an iPhone or similar product you can take photographs and shoot video. There are talented people shooting shorts and feature films on camera phones with impressive results. If you are keen to be a cameraman then you should be carrying a camera with you all the time. Use all your spare time to hone your skills and build a portfolio.

In my day a CV was one or two sheets of paper (yawn): now you can have a website and can showcase your talents to the planet. You will need to prove to a prospective employer that you are keen, dedicated and have talents and ideas to be nurtured. Broadcast your videos on YouTube or Vimeo – there's a world of critics out there. If you get even a few thousand hits then you are reaching the same audience size as some TV channels – this is CV-worthy. If you aren't getting that many hits then maybe your content isn't that great: work on it.

My advice is not to follow in my footsteps but instead create your own path to where you want to get to in your career. Be prepared for it to take time and keep you broke. The rewards are in doing what you are passionate about, and not what you *think* would be a nice career.

Sandesh V. Kadur
Wildlife Film-maker / Photographer
Felis Creations / Gorgas Science Foundation / UTB / TSC

Mountains of the Monsoon – BBC Natural World/Animal Planet –
Cameraman/Presenter
Secrets of the King Cobra – National Geographic – Cameraman/Co-
Producer
Wild India – 3-part series for National Geographic – Cameraman 1st
episode
Cats from the Clouds – Clouded Leopard doc (National Geographic) –
Cameraman/Presenter

 I am currently based partly
in the US with the Gorgas
Science Foundation, and
partly in India. At the
Gorgas Science
Foundation I help further
their work on conservation
through education. For the
last few years, however, I
have been working
extensively in India,
recording the rich
biodiversity of the country
in the form of
documentaries for
National Geographic,
Discovery, BBC and Felis Creations – a company I founded a few years
ago that creates conservation awareness through the use of visual arts.

Ten years into film-making and it still feels as if I am just getting
started! The myriad forms of nature have always fascinated me but it
was not until my father handed me his twenty-two year old Nikkormat
stills camera that I took to documenting what I was seeing. Initially
photography was a tool that I used to document my brief encounters
with wildlife in the urban sprawls of Bangalore, a city in the southern
part of India. The idea was to capture everything on camera and then
use the images to identify the living forms. With the passage of time, I
became acquainted with the technicalities of using the camera and the

basics of lighting, aperture and shutter speed. This experience was to open a new chapter for me.

In 1997 I moved to Texas to pursue higher education and got an opportunity to work with John Bax, a well-known cameraman. I assisted him with his project on the Western Ghats of India, the region that I call home. A couple of days before the proposed journey was to begin, John changed his mind, depriving me of my first opportunity to work with a professional cameraman. This was when Lawrence Lof, Director of the Gorgas Science Foundation and my long-term mentor, offered me a chance to replace John on the project. I was more than ecstatic! Immediately I dropped out of college and set out to look for equipment that would be required to make the film. Having no previous experience with film-making did not deter me from diving head-first into the ocean. I knew that once I took the plunge there would be no turning back. Ever since it has been a long hard swim and there's been no rest for the weary. I learned film-making the 'old way', in the field, 'doing'.

Technological advances had a lot to do with my getting into wildlife film-making. By the mid-1990s the advent of digital video technology brought with it many advantages. For one, it made it much more affordable to make films. The industry standard at the time was 16mm film and the equipment, lenses, and cost of post-processing were exorbitantly high. Digital also meant immediate feedback, which to a beginner is very important. One can correct mistakes while in the field and not have to wait months after the shot has been taken.

With new technology also came new cameras, some even with interchangeable lenses such as the Canon XL1, which very rapidly became the camcorder of choice for most wildlife film-makers about a decade ago. With my background as a stills photographer I found this camera perfect, as I could fit my stills-camera lenses on it and shoot video with the added advantage that the lens was 'magnified' by a factor of 7.2. So a 400mm lens translated to a 2,880mm lens, which for wildlife film-making was an absolute boon.

Apart from advantages in the field, digital also brought with it a series of software developments that allowed you to edit on your own computer. So the high costs of post-production were also reduced. Thus I spent many tedious hours experimenting and learning one of the most essential components of film-making – the art of editing.

When I first started to edit, I noticed that the shots I thought beautiful were just not binding together. That is when I realised that, as a photographer, I was always after that perfect shot, but as a film-maker what I needed instead was a perfect sequence. I still believe that that is the most important distinction between photography and film-making. Although they are related because of their visual nature, they require completely different thought-processes.

The switchover to digital was just the beginning. Over the ensuing ten years every film-maker has had to stay abreast of changes in technology. It has been more important than ever to keep up with the wave of innovations coming out and be able to grasp quickly the knowledge to use new tools and deliver creativity in story-telling. This to me has been the most challenging yet exciting part of being in this field – evolve or become extinct.

Enhancement in camera technology is continuously bridging the gap between stills photography and video. Such advances led me to use the Canon 5D Mark II when filming my travels across the enchanting north-eastern region of India. The first chapter, *Kaziranga – Land of the Rhino and the Tiger*, went on to become the first wildlife documentary shot almost entirely with the new breed of HD-DSLR technology. We filmed and edited the entire documentary in a month. The film is presently being screened at venues around the world and has received several nominations for the best short film, including those at Wildscreen in the UK, and the Roscars in South Africa.

At the time the documentary was produced, none of the major broadcasters wanted to accept footage shot on an HD-DSLR. The quality and creative freedom that these new cameras offer, however, is too good to resist and already many film-makers are using HD-DSLR technology to boost the visual elements of story-telling.

I believe there is no limit to the advances in technology that we shall continue to experience. However, as a film-maker one must not forget the importance of story-telling. The fundamental importance of this can be seen in the simple but compelling story *Green* by Patrick Rouxel. It is technologically simple, but visually compelling.

My primary focus is always to educate and entertain, and to do these I constantly try to evolve and adapt the craft of capturing stories that ignite the minds and stir the souls of people around the world.

For anyone interested in stepping into the deep waters of film-making, my only advice is to practise the three Ps – have patience, passion and perseverance – and in the end it does pay off.

Darryl Sweetland
Camera Operator
Asian Wildlife Films Co., Ltd.

Worked for:
NHU Africa
Earth-Touch
Wild Touch (Broadcast SABC2)

I have spent much of the last year developing stories, looking for wildlife locations, preparing show reels and seeking funding. The most promising project is a production for Thai TV with me as both camera operator and presenter. The filming was done in April 2010, the show reel was finished by the end of June 2010, and now, a year later, we still haven't had a decision from the broadcasters: but if I get it, it will mean 52 episodes!

I have two young children, aged 11 and 6, so a quiet year was welcome. I deliberately mention this because, of all the things I have had to deal with during filming – leeches, elephants, being bitten by a pit-viper, slipping over and breaking my ribs on my camera – by far the most difficult problem has been managing family life! This was particularly acute during the previous two and a half years, when I was filming for Earth-Touch and often away from home.

My association with Earth-Touch might seem to be one of those fortuitous stories that you hear about happening to other people and wonder why it never happens to you, but I have subsequently come to feel that there is nothing fortuitous about it at all.

At the beginning of 2007, at the age of 45, I finally decided that if I was ever going to get into serious wildlife film-making I had better make it happen soon. I had done professional stills work, some writing, and a little filming before that. I had also worked for many years as a teacher, so presenting was not a problem to me.

I had considered the Wildeye weekend courses, but could hardly justify the cost of flying to the UK from Thailand for a two-day course. I searched the Internet for something longer and came up with a five-week course at the Wildlife Film Academy in South Africa. The website mentioned the possibility of internships after the course, which was what I wanted.

I booked up, flew to Cape Town, did the course – which was great – and in the last week was offered a thirteen-week internship working on a TV series. This was a tremendous experience involving everything from researching stories, setting up the shoots, filming and recording sound, and then editing the final five-minute pieces.

The end of my internship coincided with the Wild Talk Africa film

59

festival and I prepared a pitch for a film I wanted to make. It was an open pitch with a live audience from the world of wildlife film-making. I got little interest from the panel, but when I nipped out for some coffee I was approached by a lady, who had seen my pitch and mentioned it to Richard van Wyk from Earth-Touch. I met Richard, loved his ideas, and few months later I was back in Thailand doing my first ten short films for Earth-Touch, to be published on their website. By the following year I was filming most weeks for them, by which time the content was also going out daily on SABC2 as *Wild Touch*.

This work was intense to say the least, but it gave me tremendous experience in field craft and camera technique as well as on the computer side of things. For most of the time I worked alone, which meant carrying all my gear into the forest and filming, as well as recording sound and doing the links and narration. I believe this is a growing trend and anyone who wants a career in film-making should try to develop as many skills as possible. I had two spells of assistance from a talented intern from the United States, Alex Mason, with whom I really enjoyed working, and it was this experience that put into focus what I said earlier about fortuitous meetings. When you are passionate about what you do and you work hard, the last thing you need is a team member you don't like, or who complains about being hungry when you haven't finished. I'm sure I got the job with Earth-Touch, not because of what I knew or could do, but because I met Richard face-to-face. I liked his philosophy and he could see that I bought into his ideas and was 100% committed. Similarly, if I were to need someone to work with me on one of the features I am planning, it would be Alex. The lesson from this is: get out there, get to wildlife film festivals, meet people, get known, and let people see how much you care about wildlife. Your experience doesn't matter anywhere near as much as your passion and character.

For me, the biggest changes that have occurred in recent years have been to do with format. The problem is the many forms of HD and the wide range of cost associated with those different standards. I was lucky to be given a Sony 900 to use in my second year with Earth-Touch, after initially filming with a Panasonic DVCPro HD camera at a fraction of the cost. I have now purchased another Panasonic at a much higher spec and cost than my original model, but it is still DVCPro HD and therefore not acceptable to all. I worry that this camera might have a very limited life if I were thinking only of big International projects, but as an antidote have decided to concentrate my efforts on making programmes for the local Asian market, where even SD is still used.

I hope that the future of documentaries will be much more 'true' reality. I became rather disillusioned some years ago by what seemed to be a growing trend in documentaries based on laying hands on wildlife, or confronting wildlife in order to get maximum action and aggression, with the dubious justification of its being associated to some scientific research. I have come to refer to these as 'made-up-stories' – perhaps I am being over-cynical, but I do not think that the claim that 'the audience loves this kind of programme' cuts any ice. I believe there is very little we can say about what people 'like': we can only know what they have been prepared to watch, to date, out of what was on offer so far.

This should give us all hope because I really believe there are still countless stories out there to be told, and numerous ways in which to tell them. My own feeling is that there is a great hunger for raw and honest productions incorporating more and more of the behind-the-scenes material that can be done on very modest budgets and doesn't require the top-end HD equipment. In the show reels I've been making for Thai TV to consider, I filmed the wildlife with the main camera, while being followed by another cameraman filming what I do and the reactions of the children with me. It was unscripted, and we filmed what we found and really camped in the forest. Where possible I narrated while I was filming in order to get the real excitement at the moment of seeing something. It may be that this kind of true reality programming is best suited to short-form stories, available online, as in the early Earth-Touch model. Though raising revenue from online material like this seems problematic.

If wildlife film-making is your dream and you haven't yet made a start, do so right now! Search the Internet for courses. It's going to cost you money, but it may just be the best investment in your life. After the course, go for an internship. In South Africa it is common for people to start in film-making by doing a three-month or even six-month internship. Don't think of this as unpaid work, think of it as free training. Get hold of whatever camera you can afford, or borrow one. Buy or make a hide and get out into your garden, or a wood near you, and start filming. Find your own story and style. Film anything, get it into some kind of editing program and play around with it. Study how other films have been put together. Book yourself into the next wildlife film festival nearest to you and start meeting people.

Camera Assistant

The camera assistant accompanies the cinematographer/camera operator in the field and assists him/her in any way that is needed. This can include servicing cameras, taking still photographs, recording sound, downloading and backing-up files, building hides or tree platforms, constructing sets, carrying equipment, putting tents up, driving, cooking meals and so on.

Gail Jenkinson
Camera Assistant
Freelance

Atlas 4D – episode *Mediterranean basin* (Darlow Smithson Productions)
Among the Apes – episode *Gorillas* (Dragonfly Ltd)
Meerkat Manor – The Story Begins (Oxford Scientific Films/Discovery Films)

As a freelance camera assistant I work on a huge variety of productions that range from drama and documentary to natural history, drama reconstruction and underwater shoots.

I began assisting in television after working as a photographer's assistant. But photography was not for me: I was often in a studio, I wanted to work within a larger team, and I definitely needed to spend more of my working day outside. My photographic background has been useful though, and it's a skill that crosses over well, so I always recommend spending time with a stills camera and honing your talents to create great composition and an interesting frame.

I enrolled on a Wildeye course and shortly afterwards bit the bullet and

62

moved to Bristol to pursue a change. I believe the Wildeye course and the contacts I made there are at the heart of my new career, and one I forged at the age of thirty-five! So I'm most certainly not fresh out of college.

I arrived in Bristol with six months' rent and it took a year and a month to gain work in the BBC Natural History Unit. I attended Wildscreen and other networking events, gaining contacts that I continue to nurture, keeping up a rapport with people in the industry so that one day – when the opportunity arrives – you are on the top of the list.

Years later and still in Bristol, it is often said to me that it's a good thing I keep throwing mud at the walls, hoping one day something will stick! For me perseverance is key: you don't read about the people who gave up, do you?

I am involved in the wildlife filming community, attending events and courses to gain new and relevant skills. Over the years, positions for camera assistants have been getting fewer and further between, but there are related possibilities including the role of the DIT (Digital Imaging Technician). But for me multi-skilling is key.

When you are working on a production with a small crew, and are living and working together, you need to be flexible and a team player. The more diverse skills you have the better. I have often been the one bandaging up a fellow crew-member after an injury, so my First Aid experience has come in handy and, I believe, contributed to my being a valued member of the team.

Future technical changes will mean making an effort to keep up to date, attending courses and trade shows when possible: but don't be put off by too much jargon, as just an understanding is useful. For me, creativity is still the ultimate skill to nurture.

Be specific, but not immovable, in the chosen area you wish to work in. There is so much to learn from drama and film production when making wildlife programmes, having diverse experience gives you a broad knowledge and greater creative viewpoint.

Finally, of course, there are very many newcomers to the business each year, new graduates entering an already over-subscribed industry; but somebody has to do it, so why not you?

Louise Purnell
Camera Assistant
Freelance

Extreme Dreams (Arctic and Kilimanjaro expeditions) BBC

I work as a camera assistant, which involves a whole range of different types of work. I have been second camera, sound recordist, mini camera and remote camera operator, driver, tent-builder: you name it. I also film and edit my own wildlife conservation films.

I first got the taste for filming when I spent a year travelling in Southern Africa. I was lucky enough to help out a family friend as a runner on a documentary about a dam in Namibia. It struck me at the time that this was a pretty great job, travelling to amazing places, seeing wildlife and meeting fascinating people.

After studying History of Art at university I decided to go back to Africa. I started fundraising to take part as a volunteer on a Marine Conservation project to Madagascar. The country fascinated me, and it was a chance to develop my diving skills. At the end of the project I decided to stay on and teach English in the local school. While I was there a film-maker came to make a short film about the coral reef: he needed some help with the underwater camera work and of course I volunteered.

By now I was hooked on the idea of working in wildlife film-making. When I got back to England I managed to get a job as a production assistant for Case.TV who specialised in educational and factual television. I worked there for a year, mainly on a series about Latin America. It was a small company so I got to see all sides of the production process. I helped with everything from logistics, like booking hotels, to research and writing scripts, but I soon found being stuck in an office didn't suit me: I wanted to be on location and behind the camera.

I started work as a technical runner in a camera hire company. This involved horrible hours and awful pay but was a great way to get an overview of all the camera and sound equipment. From there I gained the contacts and knowledge to start working as a freelance assistant.

I wouldn't say it is easy to find constant work. There are often lulls, and I think unless you are very lucky you have to be prepared for this. You need to be able to stay positive, stay focused and have the confidence that something is going to come up. Also be realistic: you might want to find some flexible back-up work for between jobs. I've found that every time I start thinking of packing it in something comes round the corner and I'm hooked again. In many ways the unpredictable nature of freelancing is exciting, but it has its down sides and it's definitely not for everyone.

In order to keep busy I have done lots of different types of camera work and taken any opportunity. I feel everything adds to your skills and you never know what one job might lead to. You may not think filming reality television shows would help film wildlife – but you'd be surprised.

As a freelancer, one of the most important skills is to keep in touch with people you meet and let them know what you are up to without overdoing it and annoying them. I definitely think it pays to have a website with up-to-date examples of you work. I have a free blog-site, which was really easy to set up, and I have even got work from people who have just Googled and found my site randomly. I find attending Wildscreen an excellent opportunity to make contacts, watch and discuss a range of films, and keep up with current trends and innovations within the industry.

Over recent years the reduction in the price of cameras and editing software means it is much easier for people to afford to buy their own broadcast standard equipment. I think buying my own camera and editing my own footage was the best learning investment. You have to be realistic about what can be achieved as a one-person operator, but with lots of planning and determination it is amazing what you can do.

To get more experience filming in the field I organised my own filming trip to South America. I brought a camera, tripod, sound equipment and a laptop with FCP (Final Cut Pro) editing software. I researched conservation projects in South America and, in particular, organisations working on marine issues (which I am particularly interested in). Then I contacted a selection of key groups, volunteering my services as a camera operator and editor with professional equipment willing to help them with their work in exchange for food and board. A number of organisations were interested.

I worked with GMTCS (Guyana Marine Turtle Conservation Society) filming advertising and publicity material to promote their initiative, developing products made from crab wood oil as an alternative income source for coastal communities. I helped Stinasu, the foundation for nature conservation in Suriname, develop promotional and educational materials for Brownsberg National Park, Galibi Nature Reserve and Matapica Sea Turtle beach. Having gained access to these areas, and contacts in the area, I was also able to film extra footage for my own films.

One of the most rewarding things about this filming was that the programmes were making a difference to conservation in the area. It was fantastic to know that the films were to be shown to the local people who rarely see their environment through the eyes of the camera. I have subsequently got involved with helping to put together the FFC (Filmmakers for Conservation) database of films that make a difference and also with GAFI (The Great Apes Film Initiative), a charity working to educate people in remote areas about conservation by screening films about endangered animals in their area. I think projects like these, which focus on constructive use of wildlife film, are really important for the future of wildlife.

Sound Recordist

Location sound is sometimes recorded by the camera operator at the same time as filming, but better results are usually achieved when a specialist sound recordist is used (or sound mixer as they are known in some countries).

The sound recordist will operate a variety of equipment to capture the sound – recorders (usually file-based these days), a variety of microphones for different applications, parabolic reflectors, boom arms etc. The sound may be recorded on to a separate audio recorder, or be recorded on to the camera's sound tracks – in this case the sound recordist will operate the microphones and a small mixer, which then feeds into the camera.

Jonathan Andrews
Production Sound Mixer & Sound Supervisor
Alien Sound Inc

Expedition Alaska with Indus Films
War Dance with Shine Global Films
Hillbilly Hand Fishin' with Halfyard Productions

Heat ribbons spun over the Oklahoma soil as if with purpose when I entered cold river-water for the first set up. While I didn't need a thermometer to know it was hot out, I also knew that I might shiver if I became chilled, and shake the fully-extended boom pole: so I thought carefully before declining to use rubber waders against the cold.

Now I'm glad I left the waders in the box. At the moment I'm wading neck-deep in the muddy waters of the Red River in Southern Oklahoma and there's no telling how I'd feel about walking around with a fifty-pound bag of water wrapped around my legs. Most of the time the water comes up only to my chest, but as soon as you hit a hole on the downstream side of the many tree trunks, you are in it up past your head. The bottom of the river is red clay and sand that mixes thickly with the water. Tree trunks jump out at anything that moves, tearing up your legs, if you're foolish enough to be wearing shorts, while the bottom of the river tries to tear the shoes off your feet. Carp jump all over the place and garfish charge you and bite at every other step.

Despite all this I have a full grin on my face because this is what I enjoy doing most: going places and doing documentaries on subjects that others feel you have to be crazy to do. Maybe it's from wearing magnets either side of my brain for thirty-odd years, or something that was in the water while I was growing up, but to me, this is natural. I'm a production sound mixer, and working on a show about hand fishing, for Animal Planet.

Blue and flathead catfish live here in the muddy waters on the Oklahoma/Texas border. These mighty animals run forty to a hundred pounds and build their nests in the abandoned beaver holes that are everywhere here on the aptly named Beaver Creek. It's no fun slipping into a hole expecting a catfish, only to find that the scales have gone furry and gained some big sharp teeth. I'm just glad all I have to do is keep my microphone and recorder out of the water.

The training I received at Pinewood taught me how to adapt and overcome most of the sound-equipment obstacles, and provide a good usable soundtrack for the post-production team to use to make a show. With the experience I gained in Pinewood's post-production theatres I learnt what was needed to fill out a track with natural sound, and also what can be got away with if it's easy to disguise. This, along with the outdoor skills I learnt growing up in northern Scotland and with the Marines, made me comfortable, or at least accepting of, most situations I encounter. My love of the outdoors was strengthened in the countryside around Lossiemouth where I ran wild as a child, often going bird-watching with my father on the laird's grounds, or walking in the woods or on beaches around the area. I'm now a long way from the corridors and stages of Pinewood Studios where I served my apprenticeship years ago, but despite all the changes the basic job is still the same: get great sound, keep the boom-shadow off of the subject, and try not to trip and fall into frame. Then maybe you'll get invited back for the next job.

In the past ten years all my life experiences have come together to give me a hobby that pays me a wage, as opposed to a job. Working in the field is where I'm happiest. Whether it's in the deserts of Morocco, the depths around Palau, the top of Mount Rorima in Venezuela or the Red River of Oklahoma, it doesn't matter: there is sound everywhere. When people sit quietly for a while it's fantastic the noise that nature makes. The sound of silence is amazing in its complexity and variety.

Over the thirty years that I've been working as a sound recording professional I have seen a great many changes. From recording a mono-track on a Nagra 3 to the introduction of the stereo Nagra, then DAT, then more recently the best advance in wildlife/expedition sound: the hard disk recorder. Computer-based recording has completely changed the way I work. With the ten-second pre-roll I can walk into the field and set myself up (so long as there isn't a cameraman or producer around). Then, once things have settled, I just have to wait for what I want to record to happen, hit record and I have it all. Nothing is missed nowadays.

I remember one time in particular: I was given a Holophone, which is a 7.1 surround-sound microphone array that looks like a Rugby ball. I walked into the forest of Southern Nicaragua and waited for the troop of resident howler monkeys to show up. An hour later the group above me got comfortable and I was able to record their activities. Suddenly, two other groups approached and the monkeys let rip with their territorial cries. The sound was phenomenal and really filled out when played back later in the studio. Thanks to the pre-roll, none of it was lost at the beginning of the track. It's at times like this that I am rewarded many times over for spending days of tedium in uncomfortable places.

The other thing about the hard disk recorders is their ability to multi-track. It used to be only in feature films that a mixer would think of sending iso (isolated) tracks to post-production as well as a mix. With the advent of the DSLR and prosumer cameras being used more and more [prosumer meaning pro-active consumer, ie not high-end kit but better than an average amateur camcorder], and cameramen being more and more mobile, it seems that post wants a mix sent to the camera's sound recording tracks, and a back-up of all individual tracks iso'd on to a multi-track recorder like a Deva V or 788T. This is the system I'm using on the job at the moment. A two-channel mix is being sent to the prosumer Sony Z7U camera that takes a shot of a timecode slate at the beginning of a piece, then we don't stop rolling until the story is over. Then post has a working mix and if they need to sweeten it they have all the tracks iso'd on a Deva and can add what they wish to it. It seems to be working, and with Plural Eyes (automatic synchronisation software) it should get even easier.

Another way that I have seen the sound mixer's work change is with web-based magazines like *Time*. Here the magazine will send a photographer into the field to take the photographs undisturbed, then a few weeks later the sound mixer will come along and record the ambience and interviews needed for the item. This is a peaceful way to do your job at the speed that is needed to get the best sound possible. When working with a cameraman you don't always get the chance to get your microphones into the best position for sound – it's a compromise. But when working alone it's done on your time, and it's all about how good you are at optimally placing your microphones.

This process is getting easier and easier thanks to the work being spearheaded by the company Zaxcom with their integrated wireless systems. Their radio microphones now communicate with each other and everything is backed up at the transmitter, all units being linked with a common timecode. We have recently done a job in Morocco where there were places we couldn't send a sound operator. So the on-camera talent wore Zaxcom transmitters that recorded everything spoken when out of range of a receiver. As soon as they got back into range it was back to the usual format with everything being recorded through a mixer. This isn't a replacement for the sound mixer (although some producers will look at it like that) but a good tool when the situation demands it. With the way the people at Zaxcom are listening to sound mixers, their gear is going to jump ahead in leaps and bounds. This will spark innovation in other companies and the envelope, once again, will be pushed.

Sound Devices now have an app that allows you to use an iPad or iPhone to control their 788T recorder. This is great near water: now you can tie the recorder up in a dry-bag and control it with the iPad in a water-resistant bag (through which it can be operated). If the iPad falls in the water or gets wet it's only $500 lost and not $15,000 plus.

As a mixer, working near the top of my game as I hope, it's my job to stay on top of this emerging technology and push ahead with it. It's important to stay on the front-edge of innovation. As soon as you lean back on your heels there are twenty other people passing you from behind. As a mixer our job is to listen to people or sounds as we record them and make sure the quality of the recording is the best it can be. It's also our job to listen to the young PA (Production Assistant) or runner, fresh out of school, as they may have the small piece of information that becomes the next big thing in the recording world. People laughed at the DAT (Digital Audio Tape) Recorder, but look how long that 'flash-in-the-pan' stayed around.

To anyone thinking of becoming a sound mixer, my first question is "why?" There is more money and more glamour in camera operation. To be a good cameraman, all the sound you need to know is 'hire a good sound mixer'. To be a good sound mixer you have to love recording sounds. Its lonely work that few people notice until you record something badly. However, we are the unsung heroes of documentary television. If you have an awesome sound-track it can be used anywhere over any shot. We don't need a good shot to sell the scene. If the sound is bad then a lot of the time the shot is also no good. If you are doing sound just to fill in as a friend of the cameraman then you are not doing the best job the sound-track deserves.

I've worked with a lot of the best documentary and expedition sound mixers from around the world and they all have one thing in common: a passion for recording sound for the fun of it. If you're not crazy then being a soundman will turn you crazy, but the rewards are enormous. What other job in the world allows you to record a pod of whales bubble-net feeding then have them erupt feet from the boat you're in, or have a troop of monkeys throw their faeces at you just because you're there under their tree, or have the joy of watching the condors sail over the Andes while you're recording the air. To me that's living.

Presenter

A presenter helps provide the viewer with a link to the wildlife – explaining what's going on, perhaps embodying a voice, providing scale, and just lending authority by 'being there'. Some presenters are specialists, or actors, or ex-camera operators. Others combine several roles – there are producers and cinematographers who also present programmes.

Presenters need to be calmly able to do several things at once: remember what they are saying, how to say it, where they are looking, and whether they should be smiling; they might be holding an animal, or walking while looking at the camera, and being aware of the producer/director making hand signals and so on.

Styles of presenting – indeed whether there should be a presenter at all – are subjective matters, constantly being debated and changing. Blue-chip style programmes with no on-screen humans were for a period (still are, in many cases) the favourite with both viewers and film-makers. Then it was deemed essential to have a lively presenter to be as hands-on with the animals as possible. Producers feared the days of blue-chip films were over, but currently they are doing well again. We shall, no doubt, continue to see these rises and falls in the popularity of presenter-led programmes and styles of presenting.

**Steve Backshall
Presenter / Author
Freelance**

*Deadly 60
Lost Land of the Tiger / Volcano / Jaguar
Expedition Borneo / Alaska*

To a certain extent my involvement in television was a mistake. Far from always wanting to be on screen, as a child I dreamed of being an author. By my early twenties I was writing for the Rough Guides, and had been published in every major paper in the country, but had underestimated how hard it would be actually to make a living at writing! Having had an idea for a television series, I took myself out to Colombia with a handycam, and filmed a pilot. I sent it to just about everyone in television in the UK, and miraculously was taken on by the National Geographic Channel as their 'Adventurer in Residence' and producer. For five years I travelled the world filming wildlife and adventure documentaries, many of which were self-filmed and edited. Some were atrocious, but it provided a steep learning curve.

Spending time in every area of production in this early part of my career was essential; having to watch my own annoying tics and imperfections over and again in the edit suite drove them out of my presenting. It also helped with finding out what shots, and elements to a narrative, were essential. Doing cheap television was also a real bonus: I learned how to make the most of a piddling budget, and how to be always honest about my methods, for example showing the moments when I was refocusing, or setting up the camera, which would normally be edited out. Making a feature of roughness ensures that you do not find yourself competing with big money productions, and that you get judged for your own merits. It also enhances the sense of reality, and while obviously there is always an element of artifice as soon as anything is filmed, I take great pride in my programmes being as honest and real as is possible.

Additionally I always followed the advice of my first boss at Nat Geo, Bryan Smith, who told me I should never try and 'present' (ie if a piece to camera feels as if it should end "This is Steve Backshall, BBC News, Croydon" then you have gone too formal), but instead should chat to the camera as if talking to my mates at the pub. It's something that I feel sets the best presenters apart, as it includes the viewer in your gang, and additionally is easier, as you're just being yourself!

After my time at Nat Geo I moved to the BBC's Natural History Unit, where I have been ever since, taking up a position as a director and presenter on the *Really Wild Show*. When that came to an end I went on to be naturalist on their many expedition series. In more recent years, I have been the wildlife expert on *The One Show*, done a kids' version of *Springwatch*, and finally got my own shows in the shape of *Deadly 60*,

73

Natural Born Hunters, *Deadly 360* and *Live and Deadly*. I've written a whole bunch of books, and have four more in the pipeline, including *Looking for Adventure* with Orion publishers.

In my more recent programmes I have formed tight relationships with my exceptional camera/sound teams, all of whom are capable of filming both wildlife and documentaries, and most of whom are qualified to climb and dive as well. We function without scripts, and with limited game-plans, confident enough in each other that we can just run with whatever happens! We try not to set up animals or situations, and if we do we are completely up-front about it. We usually have a second camera, which features not only me, but my crew and how they are doing their job. This is something that the audience seems to love; after all, if I'm dangling inside a glacier trying to hammer my axes into bullet-hard ice, there's a cameraman alongside me doing the same while holding a twelve kilo HD camera; they are the best in the world in their fields, and their exploits are often much more interesting than mine!

The most common question I'm asked is, "How do you get to do a job like yours?" Well my answer to that is far from clear-cut. The closest to a normal route is to learn the subject inside out, get a biology degree then apply to the Natural History Unit as a researcher. Once you've got your foot in the door let your series producer know of your aspirations. It sounds tenuous, but is how such illustrious talents as Charlotte Uhlenbroek, Nick Baker, Miranda Krestovnikoff, Mike Dilger and Kate Humble made their way on to the screen. For Chris Packham, Gordon Buchanan and Simon King it was through first becoming successful cameramen. For me it was doing something a bit different, which set me apart from all the many other people struggling to break into this insanely competitive field. There are tens of thousands of scarily talented people trying to crack it every year: your only chance is to make yourself stand out.

However, a word of caution: even if you are exceptional, your chances of success are slim to none. And once you have broken into television, it is frighteningly fickle and has no loyalty whatsoever. I have sacrificed everything to get to where I am, working 365 days a year, yet know for certain that all it will take is someone who doesn't rate me to come in at the top, and within months I'll be yesterday's news. This is not a career path for anyone who wants security, or 'quite fancies' getting into wildlife television. It wrecks and ruins countless people for whom it is their only dream. Be very, very certain that this is what you want before you expose yourself to potential heartbreak. However, if you do decide to plunge into this sublime industry, I can promise you a life of adventures and experiences beyond your wildest dreams; I've been to 101 countries, and in the last week have hand-fed wild spotted hyenas, filmed the world's rarest canid hunting, and sat among canine-bearing geladas in the mountains of Ethiopia. Sometimes I wake in the morning and have to pinch myself to make sure it's not a big crazy dream.

Nick Baker
Naturalist / Broadcaster
Freelance

Really Wild Show (BBC 1)
CBBC Springwatch
Nick Baker's Weird Creatures (Channel 5/Animal planet/Granada international)

How I got started: it was sort of an accident. Despite having always had a passion for natural history and a certainty that I would work with wildlife in some aspect, I had never entertained the potential of working in the media. On leaving university I started to work as a field assistant on a research post, trying to understand the life history of a rare butterfly, the High Brown Fritillary, on Dartmoor. I shouted loudly about how important this work was, which led to various interviews for local press, TV and radio. One journalist, Kelvin Boot from the then Radio 4 *Natural History Programme*, encouraged me to go further. At the same time, being a founder of the Bug Club, I was getting a bit of media interest in this project as well.

Friends in the Devon Wildlife Trust pushed a flier my way that mentioned that the BBC Natural History Unit was looking for new presenters. I made a rubbish showreel with my then girlfriend and got the job! Although I didn't really understand TV back then I took a post as a researcher for the *Really Wild Show* – and a combination of factors led me towards my first break as a presenter of this show.

The industry has changed hugely in the last ten years: so many more outlets for natural history content are available. When I started there were four UK terrestrial channels and the competition was much less, budgets were generally bigger, and nobody would dream of a crew without a soundman. And in those days a researcher would be expected to recce a shoot prior to the crew's arrival.

What has happened in recent years is that we've seen a polarisation: productions are either big-budget/blue-chip or very cheap; there is very little middle ground. We've seen an increase in multi-tasking, as camera operators are expected also to record sound. Although this is a risky strategy, the innovation and the energy that come across in these 'reality' genres can easily make up for the low production costs and in some ways make them much more exciting.

With the internet and increasing bandwidths anyone can broadcast what they want when they want. From a presenter's point of view, with all these outlets, it is much harder to escape the general mêlée, and specialisation seems to be the key. For me this isn't much of a problem but if I were solely a presenter then I would be in trouble. Fortunately I have my expertise to fall back on: I'm a naturalist first and foremost.

The future of broadcasting is very exciting: I believe the way we watch TV will change: getting what we want when we want it seems to be the way things are going – no longer shall we be waiting for shows to be delivered, and I suspect we shall watch only what we want to watch. This may make it difficult to engage new audiences but at the same time the viewer will have much more say in what is commissioned; this is both good and bad of course.

We are beginning to experiment with 3D HD TV – which, to the uninitiated, sounds like more gimmicks. Especially in the genre of natural history, however, the output is spectacular. No more gratuitous screen-popping images: it's more like a window into which you can peer and be drawn. The unknown at the moment is the commitment of the broadcasters and the viewer who will need to invest in new technology to reap any benefits.

The big marketplaces such as the USA will continue to have quite an impact on what we shall see over here. Unless it sells in the US then any concept has a limited chance of attracting any budgets over here, which I think will limit the quality and content. The best policy for the BBC is that it should maintain a quality and home interest in the face of the flood of bought-in programming.

Advice to anyone who wants to follow this career path is make your own films, play with ideas, and understand the genre. The technology now is such that you can make the sorts of films you want to see and broadcast them; the subject is still engaging. It is so much easier to put together showreels and tout them around than it ever was. But if you have aspirations of a glamorous and lucrative career, then natural history broadcasting is not the place for you. If you care about the planet and the subject with a passion, that will push you through. In this aspect the business has the potential to generate great satisfaction, but forget the idea of becoming rich and famous!

Casey Anderson
Presenter / Executive Producer
Freelance

Nat Geo Wild *Expedition Wild*

I am currently the presenter and executive producer of the Nat Geo Wild series *Expedition Wild*. To date we have produced thirteen one-hour episodes for Nat Geo. But the trail that leads to who I am now is long, and still evolving.

I started to work in the wildlife film-making world in 1994, when I was just a teenager. Growing up in the Montana wilderness I had acquired great knowledge of the animals that lived alongside me, and that knowledge was valuable to wildlife documentary producers. I was hired often for my wildlife tracking skills, not to mention my ability to carry heavy backpacks filled with camera equipment. I spent countless hours with small crews filming some of the most gorgeous animals in the most beautiful places on earth.

77

But my trail had a dark side too. During my college years I took a job as an animal keeper/trainer for a company that hired out their animals for film and television work. It was a dream come true and here I gained quite a different perspective. I got to know the various animal species – that I already knew so well in the wild – on a parallel level. I gained great knowledge and appreciation from my day-to-day interactions with each individual, something I would never gain from my observations in the wild. But back in those times ethics would be compromised for content and my dream job became a nightmare.

A deer carcass was placed in a pristine setting. A pack of captive wolves was allowed to begin to consume it. The pack's dynamics would erupt. Growling, snarling, and fights would break out, all being captured by the film crew that surrounded the scene and had commissioned the entire situation to be filmed 'as wild'. Then a wolverine was brought in a kennel and released near the site. What happened next was like a tornado of fur, blood, and teeth. It made great content for the show, but at the expense of the animals I had grown to love. Now my job was to break up the fight, stitch up the wolves' wounds, and catch a cranky wolverine who had now brutally taken over the carcass. I learned a lot about animals the hard way. After these adrenaline-filled moments of the unthinkable I would find myself back in the mountains watching wildlife from afar, reflecting on the horrific event, looking at my own scars, and learning from them. As my own wounds healed, so my evolution continued.

After a few years my developing ethics trumped my desire to make money working hands-on with animals every day: I knew it was time to leave this dark world behind. In the interim I started consulting wildlife parks on proper husbandry techniques, and wildlife training, capture, and handling. I certainly had plenty of experience by then. And all along I continued to guide film crews into the wild in search of fleeting moments. I was a hybrid in the making, learning so much along the way from both sides of the cage. But these parallel worlds functioning simultaneously were making me into the ultimate hypocrite.

I realized that I was against captive wildlife in general. In a perfect world all animals would be able to live in the wild. I also realized that we do not live in a perfect world and that some of these animals have no choice. In 2002 I founded the Montana Grizzly Encounter: a rescue and educational facility that rescued grizzly bears from horrible captive places and gave them a wonderful permanent home, all while educating the public about co-existing with the rescued bear's wild cousins. It seemed like a perfect model of compromise for my inner turmoil and hypocrisy. Soon several wonderful grizzly bears were removed from abusive situations to become ambassadors to the thousands of people who would come to see them. The visitors, who either lived in or were traveling through the Yellowstone region, learned how they could coexist with the grizzly bear. It was an imperfect harmony, yet it was extremely effective in changing people's minds. Why not use this model for wildlife films?

In my free time I am a connoisseur of my trade and I watch wildlife films regularly. I am a purist. I prefer shows without hosts and with minimal narration. I like beautifully boring films; the type that preaches to the choir, the type whose audience is people like me, the people who already care. But as I got more and more involved in producing, I realized that in order to make films that will make a difference to the wild world it was time for me to stop producing shows that I would watch.

In order to recruit the masses of people who did not yet care, it was time to make wildlife films that were educating and entertaining at the same time, *edu-taining* if you will, a model that seemed to be so effective at the sanctuary. And that is where I am now in my evolution. Our audience today recognizes deceit. They like genuine moments, they like the truth. Often the raw behind-the-scenes footage is more compelling than the orchestrated final product. But, in the fast-food world we live in, it must be entertaining, especially if we are to recruit the new generations and progressive cultures we need support from to protect all that we love as wildlife film-makers. But the wildlife film-maker's challenge remains as always: **never** compromise ethics for content.

In a recent episode, we film from a distance as several wild grizzly bears roll massive boulders over in search of moths to eat. To put the model into play, I then return to the sanctuary, and, as part of the captive grizzly bears' daily enrichment program, we weigh some boulders and place food under them to replicate what we have seen in the wild. The boulder weighs a ton, and Brutus the bear rolls it over with ease as I stand next to him in awe, delivering lines about grizzly bear behaviour. *Edu-taining*. And at what harm? Many people believe that working close to wild animals on television gives the audience the wrong idea. I believe our audience is smarter than that. Despite the frequent disclaimer of "Never try this yourself, I am a professional", I think the audience understands that. I believe they appreciate the honesty of the delivery and gain a different perspective, a valuable lesson. They fall in love with Brutus the bear, the fall in love with the grizzly bear, they want to make a difference for the things that they love. These people would have never watched the program if it did not have a man standing next to a giant grizzly bear.

It is my hope that some day the sanctuary will become extinct, and that the world will fall in love with all that is wild. Zoos and sanctuaries will no longer remain, and all the animals will be running free. Until then, as wildlife film-makers, we have the responsibility to be the voice for the voiceless. We must evolve, be progressive, and follow the trends in order to be effective and to reach out to the people we need to make care. Film-makers will always struggle and be critical about others' practices, but one thing we should never do is lose sight of why, and for what, we are doing this.

Scriptwriter

Constructing the story in words is a very valuable addition to the film: it can change the whole experience for the viewer, providing tension, fun, drama etc. Producers sometimes write their own scripts but, unless they are skilled writers, they often need a professional scriptwriter to go through and make improvements — known as 'polishing'. If the budget allows, it is better to work with a professional scriptwriter from the start.

Scripts for a presenter to speak will be written during the pre-production and production phases, while those for the narrator can be written beforehand as part of the story-building exercise, or after shooting when the writer knows what footage is available.

The writer needs to research the subject thoroughly, immerse himself/herself in the film, and work with the producer and the editor to provide a well-paced script with the suitable/necessary amount of information and dramatic content.

Jenny Devitt
Director – Baobab Productions
Freelance Scriptwriter, Producer and Narrator

Eye of the Storm: series for ABC (Australia) and Channel 4
Jewels of the South and *Secrets of the North*: BBC
Guy Pearce's Ultimate Guide to Tigers: Universal Studios

I began specialising in writing for wildlife documentaries just over twelve years ago, more by accident than design, when I arrived at Partridge Films in London, from France, to assistant-produce two films: one on the Camargue, and the other on the wild inhabitants of one of the grandest of French châteaux, Chambord. I'd been working as a freelance journalist in Paris, covering all sorts of topics for radio, but my heart was always in wildlife. Not surprising: I grew up in the bush on Zimbabwe's border with Mozambique, and all sorts of fascinating and endearing creatures wandered by, or hung around, or could be stumbled across any day or night of the week. Such joys in the natural world never leave you.

Partridge was one of those greats whose name had spread far and wide, so when a chance meeting with Michael Rosenberg at Wildscreen in 1988 led to an offer of a contract, I did the proverbial, and leapt at it! I shall always be immensely grateful to Michael for this break. My series idea was, I'm sure, slightly barmy, and so never materialised as TV programming, but Partridge offered plenty of opportunity. The scriptwriting partly came naturally, because I'd been writing all my own radio features and documentaries – though 'writing to picture' was a whole new ball-game.

It was the producer of the two French shows, Mike Birkhead, who suggested that I have a crack at writing them. And so there we were, my area of specialisation in wildlife filming was launched. Among the many other wildlife documentaries I went on to write were several more films for Mike, which he was producing for the BBC Natural History Unit, and

81

also *The Ultimate Guide to Tigers*, a factual tie-in for a feature film for Universal Studios, made by French director Jean-Jacques Annaud. That was fascinating, and fun, and involved a research trip to western France to interview the man who'd trained the tigers for Annaud's film. I sat, sweltering in 45 degrees of heat, on the edge of a full-sized reproduction Roman arena, while he put some magnificent lions through their paces – 'eating' some hapless Christians on the scorching sands of the area.

Things have changed, significantly, over the last six or so years for the freelancers who used to find regular work writing for wildlife films – at least in the UK. The BBC NHU was a great source of work, but then budgets began to be squeezed, and writing was increasingly seen as somewhere that savings could be made. Goodbye and farewell writers ... . Producers were expected to be able to write their own films (and find the time in the hectic final weeks or days of post-production to do so), with greater or lesser degrees of success. Some clearly had recourse to the handbook of well-worn clichés: "safety in numbers", "under cover of darkness", "stunning", etc.

etc. – need I say more? Some – oh woe! – clearly had a real talent for an original turn of phrase or expression.

Clearly it was a dangerous time to stick to just one thing. I broadened my horizons, bought a small semi-pro HDV camera, the latest Apple laptop, Final Cut editing software, and got stuck into making my own short, non-broadcast films. I always loved editing sound when I worked in radio, and editing picture and sound I found to be even more fun. I learned a lot when I went back – briefly – to France and made a documentary about how life would have been in one of the most spectacular of the Cathar castles of the Languedoc when it was built in the early Middle Ages.

Speaking personally, I'm still broadening my horizons: I now do more voice-over work, and I'm about to embark on writing my first radio play – nothing to do with wildlife: it'll be a wartime romance – plus taking the development of some ideas for children's wildlife series a stage further. So: I read (out loud), I write, I can film, edit, produce and direct. However, I have no pretensions to being either an expert camera-person or editor: a bit of a Jill-of-all-trades, you might say. I think that's not a bad route to follow, given the speed with which technology develops, and will surely go on developing.

I still love writing for wildlife films, but am adapting, as many others are doing. In classic wildlife terms, it's a survival strategy! It is a cliché to say that these are exciting and challenging times for wildlife film-makers. All the new toys in the technology shop are so much more accessible to so many more people: affordable, easier to use, lighter to carry – and you can do 'most anything from the comfort of your own home. Scriptwriters largely did, and do, that anyway, so not much change there. We can all be broadcasters and programme-makers – but the big question remains: how to make a living doing it? The internet has changed everything. 3D is the big buzz now – but will it narrow the margins of the wildlife film world yet further? Will it be a bandwagon with only a short way to run? The industry seems to be polarising: the hyper-costly blockbusters on the one end, and the DIY YouTube accessible-to-trillions mini-productions on the other. Will we all evolve immensely flat bums from so much sitting on them in front of screens?

How to break into scriptwriting for the industry? Determination and determination and determination. Enthusiasm, some good ideas, a lucky break, meeting and convincing the right person or people, and creating the right opportunity. Oh, and it would help to have a real way with words: know how to use them to best advantage to complement, not swamp or kill, the pictures you are writing for. Technology will change, but a skill with words will not. Jargon and trendy terminology will change, but their use in a wildlife script will not have as long a shelf-life, nor as much impact, as one that draws on a real love of, and feel for, our poetic and descriptive language.

Sue Western
Writer / Script Editor / Story Consultant
Freelance

The Bear Family and Me   (3 x 60' series for BBC1) – Script Executive
Lost Land of the Tiger   (3 x 60' series for BBC1) – Script Editor
The Natural World – script editor/producer/writer for over twenty-five films in this award-winning BBC2 series
Meerkats (90' cinema release, The Weinstein Company/BBC Films, narrated by Paul Newman) – script editor/co-writer

The picture-making end of wildlife films just gets better and better: images are crisper, tiny cameras show plants and animals in revelatory ways, and cameramen/women push themselves to the limit to bring back jaw-dropping shots from ever-more remote locations. In fact the bar is *so* high, the demand for the wow-factor *so* voracious, that it might seem an impossible industry to break into. But don't despair! A film should be more than the sum of its shots and sequences, and that's why good storytelling can turn even a low-budget film into a very special experience.

It was this revelation – offered up at a story-structure seminar while I was working at the BBC Natural History Unit – that gave *my* career new legs and has led to the most rewarding part of my working life. Until then I'd worked as a radio producer for the London office of Canadian Broadcast Corporation (CBC), and as a TV researcher, assistant producer and then producer for the NHU in Bristol. The CBC job was lively and varied: one day I might be interviewing an ageing rocker, like Little Richard; on another, taking in a reporter's line feeds in the middle of the night in the aftermath of the Bhopal tragedy. It was fantastic experience working on short, fast-turn-around pieces that make you focus on what's important to say and what should be left out.

But what I really wanted was a job at the NHU, so when a short-term post was advertised for a researcher on a programme about Canada (part of the series *Land of the Eagle*) I applied and luckily found myself on a three-month attachment. That sounds too easy, but I'd probably done all the hard work over the previous couple of years by making a nuisance of myself: writing proposals for *Natural World*s (BBC2 strand) and submitting them for comment; offering up ideas to NHU radio programmes (yes, at least one of the ideas got nicked) and, crucially, by completing some research for a producer who was looking for locations to film musk ox (I was living in Canada at the time). The three months turned into seventeen years.

The highlight was producing a *Wildlife on One* (BBC1 strand) on orangutans – the first time anyone had been foolish enough to try filming them completely in the wild. While at the NHU I was fortunate to be sent on the director's course at Elstree, which I found very scary, but which revealed that I had a modest talent for writing drama. It was a seminar with Hollywood script-guru, John Truby, that made a light go on in my head. I was hooked and (now also juggling the competing demands of small children) I decided to go freelance so that I could more fully combine this love of writing/structuring films and natural history.

You'd think that telling a good story would be second nature – something we learn on our parents' knees – but it seems surprisingly hard to get it right in wildlife films. I've worked in the industry for over twenty years and I can count, pretty much on one hand, the number of people who've mastered 'story'. I'm one of those still learning, but each time I'm asked to help structure a film, fix a film that's not working, or edit a commentary, I'm reminded that it *should* be a struggle. Only by applying real rigour, and asking tough questions of each shot and sequence, does the film become the best it can be. Only then can all the elements work effortlessly together.

It always amazes me, how reluctantly people commit story to paper during production, how relatively rushed the scriptwriting becomes, and how constant is the cry "we have nothing left in our budget". In an age of austerity and shrinking budgets I think it makes *ever more* sense to employ a story-writer or consultant, or to invest in a top notch story-telling course. It pays off: thousands of pounds can be saved by working out which sequences in a treatment are never going to make it into the film simply because they're 'off-message'. It's a vital process of paring down, of getting to the heart of a film, and of less being more. In the end, a final commentary script is not really about the words: it should be the minimum of fuss delivering the maximum emotional impact.

I have secretly spied on Sir David Attenborough at many commentary recordings. As the writer or producer, I need to keep an eye on the paper script, but it's hard *not* to look at the great man through the soundproof glass, because it's a chance to see a true genius at work. David turns humble words into performance art. He makes expansive gestures, raises his eyebrows, shrugs his shoulders; his whole body is physically engaged in recounting the tale. What's even better is that, although the TV audience will never see this, they can *feel* it. An Attenborough-voiced film draws you in, because he delivers it as if he has an audience right in front of him; a storyteller weaving magic over a crowd.

Audiences are sophisticated, and keen to be fascinated and moved. If we don't engage them in the most compelling and dramatic ways on behalf of the natural world, we'll have squandered an extraordinary opportunity.

Picture Editor

The picture editor's job is very important and highly creative. They are responsible for expressing the director's narrative structure – taking all the footage and choosing which bits to include or reject, and what order to put them in. They will also apply any post-production special effects to the images to enhance the production.

Editors have to be great storytellers and have a thorough understanding of the subject and the techniques at their disposal. There may be hundreds of hours of footage to sift through before choosing which sequences to include, requiring a systematic approach and an excellent memory. Whichever computer platform and editing software the editor uses, they must have a thorough understanding of its functions and complexities.

The picture editor may work alone, or more usually at least with the producer/director, and possibly together with the dubbing mixer. Major projects may have a number of picture editors overseen by a supervising editor. A series may have a series editor who oversees the editing of each programme to ensure it is in keeping with the feel of the other episodes.

Alan Miller
Editor / Director / Writer
Freelance

Baboons With Bill Bailey (Editor)
National Geographic's *Brutal Killers* (Editor/Writer)
African Bambi (children's feature · Director/Writer/Editor)

So what does an editor actually do in the post-production process? This is what it feels like most of the time: in essence, I sit at a computer, push all the right buttons (and a few wrong ones, undo and hit the right ones again) and after a few weeks what once was a cupboard full of HD tapes is converted into a single programme that will make a rapt audience smile, gasp and – in the best-case scenario – cry. As a wise commentator on our business once said, "If they cry, you've got 'em." The more elegant cliché about my primary job is the answer to how the sculptor sculpted the elephant; "I chipped away everything that wasn't elephant." That's what I do too. I take away material or promote other material in an attempt to fashion a narrative. It's the oldest form of storytelling, but with a computer in place of a campfire.

Sometimes editors have significant help (how frighteningly difficult is it to cut a feature film when the script sits in front of you? I'm certain the politics are often insurmountable, but the work is not rocket science). Often we can rely on producers and directors willing to start us off with some guidance through the jungle that is the tape-upon-tape pile of rushes. Sometimes there is almost no help. In between these two situations, it's up to you literally to make a friend, to fashion – shot by shot – a fragile (at first) form of communication that gets more robust as your ideas are played out on screen over and over again. At a certain point, that friend will tell you what it needs, and you have to serve it. Throughout post-production you will be its parent, its champion, looking after its interests, protecting it from executive producers who are busy trying to second-guess commissioning editors, making

87

suggested changes in a way that satisfies the top brass and still maintains the film's integrity. All you should care about is what's inside those four magical frame lines and how it will affect an audience emotionally. So in short, I tell stories – given the ever-more-restrictive confines of fashion, time and money.

After a BBC training in film and a few bouts of assisting on feature films, I moved to London. I'd just come runner-up in the now-defunct Lloyds Screenwriting Competition and believed (ha!) that people would simply call me and offer me writing jobs. Alas. So I walked 150 yards from my digs and found a natural history production company, fell in love with working alongside determined and passionate people, and have stayed in that general area ever since despite the seismic shifts in fortunes and futures. My true passion is film, regardless of genre, but what better storytelling education can you get? You cannot beat sixty hours of film, a Natural World fifty-minute slot to fill, animals' lives to make sense of, a merciless but talented exec and a camera-person with zero experience.

Feeling the breeze of change in the late '80s, I also became computer savvy and added a few other digital strings to my analogue bow. There are very few professionals in the TV business these days who are not hyphenates of one sort or another. When I get the chance I direct and write too but there is always a film out there somewhere that needs editing, and natural history has its own unique challenges.

Get two or more late 40s, early 50s natural history professionals together and within five minutes the conversation will turn to the good old days. And they weren't that long ago. The computer, bless, has changed everything. Those with control of the purse seem to be deluded into thinking that the faster a computer is, the faster (and therefore more profitably) the job can be done. Brains and human creativity still work as they always have. Faster computers cannot speed that process up, nor should they. This short-term thinking has buried itself deeply in natural history film-making and now a paradox has become the norm. To make programme A (an optimum *Natural World* fifty-minuter perhaps) in a mid-budget category, you needed £X, and Y number of weeks. The paradox is now the following: you are asked to make programme A (or probably expected to make a significantly more sophisticated programme A) for 20% of £X and 20% of Y weeks. It is in every practical sense unworkable and – worst-case scenario – it burns people out, people desperate to do a good job; it also makes us all appear to be chronically over-budget, and cheapens the quality of what should be a crafted show rather than a show that escapes our loving attention too soon; in the end it's the audience who suffer. Welcome to modern TV production, the way things are. The polarisation of production is staggering. It's the fiscal equivalent of that old Hollywood adage on casting: you get either Tom Cruise or Tom Smith. There seems to be very little middle ground. Now there are exceptions, organisations and individuals who still know what it takes to make programme A. And it is my wish to continue to work with people who understand the creative process and – feeling well disposed to the world – it is my wish that *you* will get the chance too (as long as I'm busy on something else).

Technology marches on and it is expected that even this year's release of the new Final Cut Pro will have seasoned professionals scratching their heads wondering why Apple have changed so many things. There are two schools of thought: first, 'new' is almost universally reviled if 'old' worked fine, but then after a week or so you can't imagine not working on the 'new'. Fingers crossed. One thing that is probably not destined to accompany us into the future of picture editing: 3D. Two years ago, *Avatar* announced boldly a resurgence and dominance of what was (and to me will ever be) a fad. The take up of 3D TVs has not been meteoric and while studios hailed it as the new 'unpirateable' format that people will pay extra to see, I can't imagine its potential ubiquity even seriously challenging traditional 2D. When everything is shot and cut, all people want is to care. Did you shed a tear after the first ten minutes of Pixar's masterful *Up*? Did the 3D elicit that tear, or was it the superbly crafted storytelling? That is an (up)loaded question.

What will be different in a decade are patterns of distribution. Expect the web to inform our lives even more than it does now, and the craft of editing will be even more necessary to make sense of the image bludgeoning we will be subjected to over and over again. And while natural history filmmakers may never get rich, you may find yourselves making more intimate programmes out of passion for a more select, web-based audience. The Internet's first wave has broken, exposing the human race *en masse* as undiscerning creatures with a knee-jerk chuckle, lying in wait for a sneezing panda. As the second wave musters itself, we can be a little choosier regarding our online education and entertainment. The movie *Green* will not be alone out there, lavishly feted by all in the know, bought and traditionally distributed by all who said "No." The most celebrated independent film of my time, and no broadcaster or distributor wanted to touch it. But the audience for it is still there.

If you are considering a career in picture-editing natural history films, then knowing the basics of animal behaviour is a must. Degrees in zoology are not mandatory, but you should know enough to avoid asking such questions as this one, asked by a producer I was working with a little while ago: "Are crocodiles evil?" I'm hoping I don't need to debate animal morality on these pages. I also worked with a young assistant who said it was her desperate desire to be a picture editor, and I asked her which editors' work she admired (it's not a trick question, it really isn't). Needless to say, she couldn't name a single practitioner of this underappreciated and subtle craft. You want to learn? If you are serious about getting to edit professionally, you need to be familiar and competent with both Final Cut Pro and Avid. If you don't know what either actually is, perhaps you're cut out for another position in the natural history film-making world.

Be sure to watch TV and film and be aware of the artifice – and be even more aware of why people almost blindly accept the artifice as true. Stand back and understand why cuts are made (and not made). Remember, editing is not a science. What may work for Jack may be despised by Jill. But you will develop your own style (I am well aware of my own quirks) and in time you will learn what we all learn eventually – the more you pick up, the more you realise that you will never stop learning. Be open, practise sound narrative judgement, listen to your own campfire Jiminy Cricket in your mind and finally, cut ... don't mix. You'll be surprised how sharp your decisions become once you banish the safety-net of mixing instead of cutting.

Oh, and have some fun!

Laura Turner
Editor
Freelance

The Wildlife Garden Project
Big Cat Film Safari (Wildeye)
The Beach Taken By The Land – Australand (CTV Perth)

I would say I'm still very much at the beginning of my wildlife film-making career, and a large proportion of my work still involves filming and editing promotional videos, live events and web videos. But as much as I can I also work as an editor on conservation documentaries, wildlife charity promos and on my own wildlife projects. Although I am primarily an editor, I've found it very useful to be able to multi-task, and so I also work as a camera operator and director, and on some occasions even as a presenter or voice-over artist!

Getting started wasn't easy – it never is! After getting my degree in Media and Video Production, I started looking for work at local video production companies. I used my holiday leave from my job in a call centre to work (for no pay) and gain experience, until eventually the work started trickling in. I quickly realised that having the ability to shoot and edit was a real bonus: being able to see a production from start to finish meant I didn't have to rely on other people for work, I could find my own. So I set up my own business as a sole trader – Ant Farm Films – created a website and started getting the word out. Work was slow to build, but I was over the moon when I got busy enough to quit my mind-numbing day job!

Once I was making my living from video production, I turned my attention to my passion: wildlife. I attended a few Wildeye courses and began looking for work in wildlife film-making. I found myself working for nothing all over again to try to gain experience and contacts. But it paid off. After applying for a job with Wildeye, I got an email that I couldn't believe: I was being invited to come and be the editor on the Wildeye *Big Cat Film Safari* in the Masai Mara! My response was obvious – I don't mind if I do!

Following this amazing experience I began getting a little more work in conservation film-making. However it still wasn't quite enough, so I decided to do something about it myself. I set up The Wildlife Garden Project (www.wildlifegardenproject.com) with the aim of inspiring as many people as possible to make their gardens wildlife friendly. The plan was to transform a garden into a wildlife haven over the course of the year and make a film of the whole thing. But I didn't want to inspire people to get out into their gardens without giving them the tools to do it, so I found some amazing volunteers who helped me set up a website with loads of wildlife gardening tips, information on garden species, a forum and updates on the film.

I think the approach that I took is a reflection of how much easier it is to go it alone these days. As technology moves on and gets cheaper it becomes easier to fund your own films. When I first started into wildlife film-making, I got the impression from a lot of experienced people in the industry that the only real way to make a film was to come up with a proposal, pitch your idea to a major broadcaster, and cross your fingers that they didn't steal it! But I heard lots of stories about people who had just gone ahead and made their own films. I knew this was the path I preferred to take, and because I already owned my own kit, I decided to go for it.

I also think that advances in technology are leading to another big change in wildlife film-making, not in the production of films, but in the marketing of them. The online presence of The Wildlife Garden Project is something I have thought a lot about. We want to get the message to as many people as possible, and through trying to provide a genuinely useful website with loads of advice, information and videos, we hope to have a reasonably  large and interested audience when our film is finished. But the key to having a good online presence rests without a doubt in social media sites like Facebook and Twitter, as well as YouTube. These are tools that have become essential to spreading the word, updating our followers, and drumming up interest – in a way that a website alone could never do.

So, if there is no one making the kind of film or spreading the message that you want, my advice would be to go ahead and do it yourself. It will take over your life, but if your idea is good then there'll be other people who will believe in your cause. I was startled by the number of amazingly skilled and passionate people who were willing to work on The Wildlife Garden Project for nothing. Then shout about it wherever you can, create a website and exploit resources like Facebook and Twitter. Let YouTube host your videos for you and you'll get more hits as people search for the particular subject. If you are raising awareness of a particular cause, give suggestions about how people can help, and give them a reason to return to your website time and time again.

If you are an aspiring editor, my advice is to practise, practise, practise! To begin with you can use a free editing programme like Windows Moviemaker or iMovie, to start building up a showreel. Offer to edit student films, work free for local video production companies, or make your own film. Try to edit a range of films: I've learned just as much from working on fast-paced flashy corporate videos as I have from heart-wrenching charity films. If you can learn how to colour grade and create graphics, even better. You'll become even more employable as companies often prefer to hire one person to do the edit from start to finish. Be prepared to go through hours and hours of footage, and to get frustrated at sitting in a dark room all day when everyone else is frolicking in the sunshine! However, there's nothing quite like that feeling when your edit starts to work, and even better when you get that tingle down your spine because you know you have created something that will invoke excitement, joy or even tears in your viewer.

Finally, remember always to give something back. If someone helps you, find a way to repay the favour. Everyone knows this industry is all about contacts, but it's even better if those contacts become your friends. Good luck!

Music Composer

Music is often overlooked, but it is an important creative element that can change the whole feel of a film. It can build tension, drama, surprise, humour, sadness, or can be relaxing or uplifting. Having said that, there is continued debate about the quantity (and quality) of music used in wildlife films – it's a subjective matter.

Music is either composed especially for a film, or the rights are obtained for existing recordings, or it is bought in as library music. Library music is usually the cheapest option – but much of it is dreadful, and it is hard work finding the right music to fit in with the film. The first choice, if budget allows, will be to employ an experienced composer.

Music can be played by real orchestras, or by a small group of musicians using conventional instruments, but increasingly commonly it is produced by a single composer using the latest keyboards and samplers. These are often used in the composer's own home studio where a computer is used to sequence the keyboards and multi-track the instruments.

William Goodchild BA (Hons) LGSM
Composer / Orchestrator / Conductor
Freelance

Production companies I've worked with include: BBC, Icon Films, Parthenon Entertainment, Aqua Vita Films, Quickfire Media, Nature Picture Library, Available Light, Lion TV.

Three productions for which I have scored the music:

Miracle in the Marshes of Iraq – BBC *Natural World* Special. (Alternative title, *Braving Iraq*, PBS Nature).
Producer/Director: David Johnson. Production Company: Aqua Vita Films.
Winner of the following awards: 2011 Gold World Medal in the Environment and Ecology category at the New York Festival's International Film and television Awards; Best in Category Award at the International Wildlife Film Festival: Best Conservation and Environmental Issue, and Merit for Conservation Message.

Wild Russia – 6 x 50 minute series for National Geographic International. Series Producer: Amanda Theunissen; Director: Dan Habershon-Butcher. Production Company: Parthenon Entertainment. Narrated by Paterson Joseph.

Lobo - the Wolf that Changed America – BBC *Natural World*.
Producer: Brian Leith; Director: Steve Gooder.
Production Company: Brian Leith Productions. Narrated by David Attenborough.
Winner of the following awards: Jury's Special Prize, Wildscreen International Film Festival 2008; Outstanding Achievement, Jackson Hole Wildlife Film Festival, 2009.

I compose and produce music for a diverse variety of wildlife film projects and have scored films for all the major broadcasters including the BBC, National Geographic International, Animal Planet, Channels 4 and 5. Projects have included scores for photographic stills promos, individual documentaries for the BBC and independent production companies, and full-scale wildlife series.

So how does the process work? Starting as early in the post-production process as possible, preferably before the edit gets under way, the director and I will discuss the project. We talk about the film's narrative, its principal characters and the geographical setting. We also discuss ideas about musical style, feel and pace. Sometimes the director will have a preference about the choice of instruments to be used! More often than not this sort of decision is left to the composer.

On the back of early discussions, I will write a theme or two for the director to hear. This is a good time to get an idea for what might and might not work for the project. I also like to produce a musical 'tool kit' for the editor to play with in the early stages of the edit: this may include one or two drones, stings, 'atmos' pieces and a theme or two. [a sting is a short musical phrase, used as a form of punctuation – for example at the end of a scene, or as a dramatic climax is imminent.] Placing music early into the edit begins a conversation between music, picture, narration and sound effects, that continues all the way through to the final mix. The more time there is for this conversation to develop,

95

the stronger and more honed and integrated the music will be with all the other elements of the film.

As the edit proceeds, the score begins to take shape: certain key sequences will require music to lead the action, others will require subtle underscore. Certain picture or narrative elements will need highlighting or accenting by music. The role of the music is to provide a subtext, to drive the story, to add emotion, to provide glue where needed, to help continuity, sometimes to help sell the film. The music is always heard in relation to the other sonic aspects of the film: the spoken narration, and effects. Awareness of these is key when scoring. The craft therefore requires huge amounts of flexibility and an instinct about when to come forward, when to hang back.

The placing or spotting of music is a vital part of the process. Decisions about when, and when not, to have music, are crucial to the pacing of the film and how it breathes. Decisions about music placement are made and re-made? from the beginning of the process right up to the final mix.

Individual broadcasters have distinctive styles musically, particularly with regard to pace and style that relates to the channel's perceived demographic. This is something that also needs to be borne in mind and taken into account when scoring a project: for example Animal Planet is faster, brasher and more pop-driven than, say, the BBC.

Having worked professionally as a musician, performing and teaching for a number of years, I met an established wildlife composer who was looking for the services of an orchestrator and conductor (orchestration, by the way, is the process of adapting, for orchestra, music composed for another medium, such as piano or electronica). I was practised in both these skills and was able to help. The first project we worked on was a blue-chip BBC series on North America with the score performed by the Royal Philharmonic Orchestra and recorded at Angel Studios in London. This went well and more projects followed. The relationship gave me an apprenticeship: I was able to observe the role of the composer within a project at first hand and begin to grasp the ways in which music can work with wildlife material. Orchestration led eventually to co-writing and finally to gaining my own commissions as a composer.

Two of the biggest changes in the television industry over the last ten years have been the development of technology and the diminishing of budgets on many projects – both due to greater competition. A composer, now, not only composes but also is required to perform,

programme, engineer, orchestrate, fix players, MD, edit, and mix – jobs traditionally performed by others within a team. Technology has facilitated this change and lower budgets have demanded it. [jargon-busting:
'programme' – organise sound electronically or digitally to construct a musical performance (rather than the performance being purely played on an instrument and recorded), 'fix players' – book players for a recording session, 'MD' – Musical Director, or conductor].

Technology has also had an impact on the picture-edit itself: because changes are easier to make, decisions can be left until later, and this can often add extra pressure on the composer whose job comes at the very end of a long production process. There is far greater fluidity on projects now, and decisions are made on the surface, often after the event, rather than before. Picture lock [when all the changes to the picture-edit have been completed and approved] is a crucial stage for the composer and it is increasingly delayed, narrowing the window for the composer to do his or her job.

A more highly-competitive market with lower budgets, combined with the facility of the internet, has also led to new ways of viewing the composer and gaining music for a film. There are often voracious attempts by production companies to hold on to the composer's publishing in order to claw back income and cover costs from mechanical and performance royalties. Royalties play an important role for a composer, providing much-needed income when projects are sparse. If royalties have to be given away in order to retain a commission, income problems ensue further down the chain. In addition, music libraries offering cheap subscription models to make music available to production companies have, in some cases, negated the need for a composer. All of this can have an impact on the quality of programming and the composer's livelihood and existence.

There is no doubt that the way music is created, sourced and exploited is changing fast. It is becoming easier and cheaper to make and produce music than ever before. Perhaps the divide between high-end and budget film-making will widen, with the former affording strong budgets for music with a composer on board, the latter utilising free or low-subscription music. Whatever changes are afoot, I have no doubt the need for a well-crafted and emotional score in wildlife film will always remain foremost in producers' minds.

To succeed as a composer you need to be really passionate about music and film. Develop your craft, concentrate on writing, and find as many opportunities as you can to practise and improve your skill. Writing for television and film calls for diversity – a big range of expression and a wide stylistic base. You'll need to be able to work fast and be infinitely flexible. A music degree with postgraduate training in music for film can be useful and it will give you a firm foundation in musical craft. However it's not the only way to get into the business: there are many highly successful composers who have not had a traditional training in music and have arrived through other routes.

You also need to make connections in the industry, particularly with producers, directors and editors. So put together a CD/DVD showreel of some examples of your work: some audio-only excerpts, and some 'to picture'. Keep things concise and show lots of variety. Remember, less is more, and quality is everything! There is also a number of excellent online organisations such as BASCA (British Academy of Songwriters, Composers and Authors) and Screened Music Network, which exist to inform and support the composer, whether emerging or established.

Having an online presence is useful. A blog is a good way to start as it's free to set up and maintain. It can be useful as a calling card or brochure. Showcase your musical work, have photos of yourself in action (if you perform) and keep a picture and audio record of any jobs you may get. Link your blog to social networks such as Twitter or Linkedin to increase your contacts. Listen and learn when you meet others.

You'll need a back-up. Try to develop a skill that will bring you into contact with musicians and other people in the industry. This can be performing, orchestrating, conducting, copying, engineering, programming or editing. Some of the big London studios like Abbey Road or Angel Studios offer placements with training – great for getting a feel as to how the business works and for making contacts. Instrumental teaching can be a useful way to earn money in the early stages and it allows for some flexibility in hours, which is something you'll need. Scoring a project requires total commitment: long days and late nights, but what happens in the gaps between projects? You'll need a fallback.

If you are serious and committed, and can think of nothing else, have a go. Work hard and persevere. With some good connections and a little luck, you can go places, but you'll need to be patient.

Orchestrator William Goodchild conducting *Nature's Great Events Live*, composed by Barnaby Taylor and Ben Salisbury, with the BBC Concert Orchestra and Sir David Attenborough. September 2009, Colston Hall Bristol. Photo by Rachel Goodchild.

Cody Westheimer
Composer
New West Studios, Inc.

The Mono Lake Story
True Wolf
Ocean Adventures

The most important aspect for any film music score, whether it be a wildlife-centric production or its Hollywood counterpart, is *tone*. When my fingers first hit the keyboard as I'm embarking on a new project will it be *Major*? *Minor*? *Suspended*? Will the sound be a *Piano*? *Harp*? *Strings*? *Exotic bells*? There are many ways to accomplish similar *moods* through harmonic language, instrumentation, tempo and more, and these are all important aspects to consider when you a score a scene in film. In

99

wildlife film, particularly, the attention to these details is magnified. If there is speech, it is quite often narration, which is a bit more disconnected from the story in comparison with a Hollywood screen star. Music can often help to bridge this gap. If we cannot read a wolf's thoughts from its face, music can give it a voice. Music is a very powerful force in storytelling. Where does the music lead? Where is the music going? The broader story-arch is often overlooked when focused on scene-by-scene. This is where musical instincts are even more important – that kind of emotion, the broader stroke, is subtle.

I first started to get serious about this music thing in my early teens. After some initial success, I decided to get my formal education as an undergraduate at USC's Thornton School of Music. Studying classical orchestration is vital for anybody who wants to write in the contemporary film scoring style(s). While attending classes I was scoring student films at USC's acclaimed cinema school. This is where I really honed my 'dramatic sense.' A composer, in my opinion, is really not that different from a say, a writer. A good writer knows when to drop in a fast-paced scene to "refocus" the audience. And a great writer knows when to have that same scene not only increase the pacing but also enhance the story-line! We composers have that same sense – but use notes instead of words.

When I first started out as a professional back in 2000, the industry was in transition. On the production side DV was coming of age, and in post-production Final Cut Pro was released. And of course major improvements were being made to DAWs (Digital Audio Workstations) such as Pro Tools, Logic, and Digital Performer. Music sample libraries were being revolutionized by software called Gigastudio, and suddenly it was possible to 'up the ante' for production value all around. The last several years have seen even more improvement in the realm of sample libraries. If you know how to orchestrate and arrange for real orchestra, it's now possible to create shockingly realistic renditions via sampling – using 'virtual instruments' – inside any up-to-date computer. Live instruments are still a key part of my workflow – I try to record acoustically whenever possible – but the latest array of samples has made it possible to provide a full-blown orchestral palette for any project – regardless of budget. It's a little scary to envision where this is leading to, as the samples are just getting better and better, and I'd imagine they'll get more and more user-friendly over time. I doubt the real orchestra will die, though – it will always exist at the highest level – it's just that production quality at the lower budgets will be much higher, which is really a big win in the end.

Tools are essential to this job – having the proper sounds, reverbs and speakers – but to be a successful composer I think the associated skill set is often overlooked and/or undervalued. Not unlike a shooter who owns a killer camera: if they can't pull focus with the big boys (and girls!) they're not as valuable as their equipment! A composer with the proper tools but an unrefined skill set will be similarly left behind. Especially in wildlife film where the budgets are often slim, you're forced to play 'one man (or woman!) band', which even further magnifies the need for a top-notch skill set. In the old days you'd just be responsible for actually writing the music – the jobs of music editor, orchestrator, copyist, recording engineer, mixer, etc went to separate people. Today it's generally *all you* – just like a film-maker producing, shooting and editing his/her own film. While you can't argue with raw talent, I truly believe the following items can be refined and learned through experience:

Dramatic Sense: eg when you're big (musically) and when you're not.

Orchestration: eg if you don't get schooled, at least buy and study a book!

Mixing: eg what *should* an orchestra sound like? How do you EQ this guitar?!

Technical Know-how: eg how to fix your computer at 1am.

While the focus is often on orchestra, 'times, they are a-changing'. Many of the scores I've worked on in the independent film world have not only been non-orchestra, but they've been anti-orchestra! The producers were actually scared of sounding too big or 'Hollywood'. This forced me to look at other ways of achieving dramatic flair without the usual crutch that is the string section. More often than not it's all about integration and blending what was the old 'Hollywood Sound' with newer, contemporary sounds. Some recent (and very successful) scores have taken the hybrid concept to the next level, to the point of eliminating melody in favor of textures and musical atmospheres. I think melody is important in many situations, but not all. Whereas 'theme' used to be synonymous with 'melody', it can now mean anything from a recognizable chord progression to a striking sound that's memorable enough to stand on its own.

If I were starting out today, I would offer this as a training plan: go to school – get a composer's degree; learn classical orchestration; score anything and everything you can get your hands on while you're in school. Then give yourself a healthy budget and buy a top-end computer and every sample library you can. Grab a nice microphone and preamp too. Start writing high-end demos that don't sound like this person or that person, but sound like you! Attend film festivals and work the crowd. Be at the top of your field sonically – your music needs to sound amazing! This way you're on a level playing field with composers higher up the totem pole (at least with regard to quality). Get the experience. Be underpaid, but build a credit list and network of loyal clients.

In the end you've got to love long hours and intense scrutiny. Film-makers typically have a very clear idea of what they want – but bear in mind that music is often the one thing they can't do themselves. Sure, they usually hire a shooter, editor etc, but they speak that language since they've typically done that job themselves. They don't always speak your musical language – it's your job to translate and adapt to their requests and needs – that's what will lead to a lasting (and usually fulfilling!) collaboration, and, let's hope, to years of success and rehires!

Post-production Sound

The dubbing editor is responsible for selecting and assembling the sounds used to create the final sound-track for the film. They may be involved in the studio recording of some of the sound – the narration and 'Foley' sound for example. Foley sounds are all those little scuffles, crunches, splashes, animal footsteps etc that couldn't be recorded for real (usually because they are very quiet or too far from the microphone at the time). In many films there is far more Foley sound than the viewer appreciates.

The live sound, extra location sound (atmospheres etc), music, narration and sound effects will all be separate recordings that have to be blended together seamlessly and creatively in the studio. The dubbing mixer comes in at the post-production stage to mix all the sounds together and produce the final sound-track. On a small project this job is occasionally done by the picture editor while cutting the footage together, but the best results usually come when a sound specialist does the actual mixing of the tracks.

Richard Crosby
Dubbing Mixer
Films at 59

Everest 1 – Tigress
DIY SOS – BBC
The Children Who Fought Hitler – Testimony Films

I'm part of a team of nine dubbing mixers and six dubbing editors who work at Films at 59 in Bristol. Our role is to create the final soundtracks for film and television productions.

Films at 59 are one of the major facilities for pre- and post-production in the UK. We supply camera and audio equipment for the initial shoot right through the editing; offline and online processes; multimedia enabling such as DVD or Blue-ray authoring; multi-format vision mastering; Hi-Definition and 3D with sophisticated multi-channel audio from mono through stereo to 5.1 surround-sound and beyond, with 7.1 and 9.1 formats possible, and specialist super-surround for exhibitions and venues such as the Eden Project.

I came to post-production sound following sixteen years in professional theatre where I worked in stage management and sound. The last eight years were working with an internationally-acclaimed dance company not only as stage manager but also as sound engineer, and, as I worked closely with the orchestra, I spent a lot of time in orchestra pits!

The nature of the work involved a lot of time on the road, and during that time I was fortunate to meet and marry my lovely wife. When children appeared the decision was taken to stop my nomadic existence and focus on my sound skills at a relatively fixed base. Following a chat with the head of film sound at the BBC's Ealing Film Studios I was offered a post as an assistant dubbing mixer in 1980. This taught me a lot about selecting or creating the right sound to match and complement the visual image, and also how to find my way around the

BBC's sound library! It also provided an opportunity to work on a huge range of programming including prestigious dramas, children's shows, current affairs, sport and documentaries.

This period also included the chance to work for BBC Pebble Mill and BBC Bristol, which gave me my first real exposure to mixing for natural history, Bristol being the home of the Natural History Unit.

In 1988 I was given the opportunity to work in Bristol for ITV, a welcome move away from London that brought me into the heartland of natural history film-making. When Partridge Films moved into the building, the chance to develop my natural history sound-mixing skills developed further.

During that period ITV were contracting: the opportunity arose for Films at 59 to acquire the dubbing operation and they did so, investing heavily in the infrastructure and new technology. I was offered a position with Films at 59, and took it!

The technology back in the 1980s was nearly all film-based, either 16mm or 35mm, with non-automated analogue mixing consoles. All pre-mixing had to be re-recorded and any subsequent changes could involve re-loading original tracks and remaking the pre-mix before continuing the final mix. Machine rooms were full of heavy engineering and labour intensive.

The advent of video as an acquisition tool and broadcast medium brought with it new challenges. Film-based audio ran alongside the video for a while and attempts to use multi-track tape recorders for dubbing gave a chance to increase the availability of tracks, as only the major feature film dubbing studios had the resources to supply the expensive multiple film machines needed. In 1988 a single 6-track 35mm sound recorder with *Dolby A* noise-reduction cost about £25K, translating to £53K in 2011 money! An Otari 24-track tape recorder with *Dolby SR* noise-reduction cost around £30K, or about £65K today. This sort of money can now buy you a pretty good *complete system* including mixing desk and Digital Audio Workstation (DAW).

Fundamental to the progress of multi-machine working was the use of timecode. This can be thought of as a digital electronic sprocket-wheel synchronising different kit together. It was developed primarily as a tool to ensure edits on the early 2" video recorders were frame-accurate. (It is an 80bit binary word comprising square wave audio bursts, 1Khz for binary 0 and 2Khz for binary 1).

Mixing consoles also started to develop automation that faithfully reproduced the inputs from the dubbing mixer. This allowed much more complex multi-track mixes to be done. Initially it was only fader, mutes and routing that automated, but this technology has moved on apace: more on this later.

The biggest revolution in audio techniques and sound manipulation came with the development of digital audio. This takes the original signal and samples it at a choice of frequencies: 32kHz, or 48kHz, up to 128kHz and beyond. The higher the sampling rate the greater the resolution. Each sample is then given a quantising level. Again, the greater number of levels allocated, the closer the representation of the original signal. This information is then translated into a string of binary 1s and 0s. The challenge facing the engineers was how to record this information. The available audio recorders did not have the bandwidth to accommodate the quantity of information generated. To start with they used video technology and an interface box allowed engineers to record audio to a Betamax video tape (hands up if you remember Betamax, a Sony domestic format!).

During the '80s, alongside the advent of digital tape-recorders from manufacturers such as Tascam, Sony, Akai, we saw the first Digital Audio Workstations (DAWs) appear such as AMS Audiofile, Sadie, Fairlight, Synclavier and Digi Design Pro Tools.

Most of the tape recorders still used a modified video technology such as helical scan spinning record/replay heads to give the bandwidth required, and expanded into multi-track formats such as the ubiquitous DA88 8-track from Tascam which developed from the Hi8 video format. The acquisition and mastering format was often 2-track Digital Audio Tape (DAT) with integral timecode that was used to synch with the camera or mixing desk.

The DAWs were developed using computer platforms. Some, like the Audiofile, used their own hardware with a closely-guarded file format. Some used PC platforms and some Apple Macs, all of them using hard disks as recording media: again, in the 1980s, incredibly expensive. To replace the drives in an Audiofile cost about £12K and that gave you only about one hour of stereo recording on about 1Gb of space!

Interchange between the offline video editors and dubbing was a bit of a headache until Avid developed the Open Media Framework Interchange (OMFI) and released it to other third-party users. All the DAW manufacturers adopted it, so a drive could be taken from the edit suite

106

and plugged into the DAW.

Mixing desks were now going digital and the multi-layer consoles gave the mixers access to a huge amount of processing. By now automation could be applied to virtually all parameters of a mix, so mixes could stay 'live' throughout the mix process; this also allowed for late changes to edits, with re-conformable automation.

By the turn of the millennium computer memory costs were starting to drop, which gave the DAW developers the opportunity to incorporate virtually unlimited tracks plus an integrated mixer within the same box. File interchange formats were expanding and now we have arrived at a virtually tapeless process in which location recorders move to hard drive or even solid-state multi-channel systems.

With the best will in the world, trying to mix a programme 'in the box' with a mouse is messy, slow and difficult if you need constantly to adjust more than one thing at a time. So DAW designers such as Digi Design with Pro Tools and Merging Technology with Pyramix (and many others) started to produce, with hardware developers, what looked like a mixing console on the outside but was actually only a manipulative tool to adjust the internal mixer built into the software. A mix can be taken from origination to any other facility with the same equipment and be faithfully reproduced.

Also, third-party software designers were developing 'plug-ins' to insert into a mix stream, which gave the sound designers and mixers huge flexibility with compression, reverbs, clean-up tools, metering and monitoring etc, all benefiting from automation, and a lot cheaper than the original hardware that inspired the software.

Credit must be given to the music industry, which was mainly instrumental (forgive the pun) in driving forward most of the development that we see now.

As the user sees a need to change the way a product operates, an email to the developer, with maybe a copy of the problem, can result in a fix being sent in very short order by way of a software patch; this is so much better than having to buy yet more equipment.

The advantage to the dubbing editors and mixers is the ability to keep options open right up to the final review. However it can also run the risk of allowing self-indulgence and loading up the tracklay with unnecessary tracks, just because you can!

The video side of things has not stood still either: from 16/35mm film through Umatic, Betacam, BetaSP into the digital formats of DigiBeta, to Hi-Definition SR formats and into 3D. They all increasingly present the ability to record multiple audio streams on the same tape. Our present HDCAM SR machines will take six 5.1 mixes, a stereo mix, and oh! unless we forget, a picture as well!

Where does that leave the future? The totally tapeless environment is with us now but the size of video files is enormous and, until data streaming gets faster, I think the final delivery format will be on tape. (The size of an average one-hour natural history project can be around 350 Gigabytes!). We do, however, mix using captured video to save running tapes all day and relocating to any point in a programme is instant.

Where does that leave dubbing for natural history?

Historically natural history producers rarely sent sound recordists out on a shoot, especially as some projects might take several years just to acquire the pictures. Also, the lens technology allows the photographer to fill the screen with a lion's head from half a mile away, at the same time not disturbing the subject: but microphone development has yet to achieve that telephoto ability.

So, frequently the audio-post team are handed a blank canvas. If we are lucky someone may have been able to record some wild-tracks of the atmospheres around the various locations. Over the years, Films at 59 has drawn together a large library of atmospheres and specific sounds, so research is critical; we can buy in sounds as required.

During preparation the producer of the programme will have had a 'spotting' session with the dubbing editor assigned to the task, where he (or she) indicates specific points that he would like worked on. Often the guide commentary also gives extra clues as to what is required.

The next stage is to create an 'atmosphere bed' on which the specific effects, like animal calls, will sit. This is where the ability to run many tracks simultaneously has its benefits: mainly that of offering options and varying the balance between shots and scenes to avoid aural boredom and to build, for example, a sense of menace or cold. The 'plug-in' also gives the editor the option to manipulate the sound in a way that a straight recording could not. At this stage the final mix format needs addressing: for example in a 5.1 mix what is going on behind the viewer can be vital to the storytelling and is fantastic at

108

fixing the geography of the sequence.

Next come the effects, which can consist of anything the editor feels would enhance the mix. This need not include just the in-vision lion's growl, for example, but also a relevant bird in the background or a rumble of thunder. This is also the time for the editor's creative skills to prevail in, perhaps, merging several sounds to create a new one. The .1 of a 5.1 tracklay can be utilised here with a sub-sonic rumble or a threatening footfall, the call of a whale or the creaking of a glacier.

Now most animals and plants move, and the inability of the microphone to capture the moment half a mile away is all-too apparent. So a 'Foley' or 'spots' recording session is needed. Here we recreate the elephant's moves, ear-flaps, dust baths, mud wallowing, tail swishing. The judicious use of a cotton glove filled with custard powder brings alive a polar bear's foray out into the winter's snow-covered landscape. The plunging of fingers into a ripe orange can turn your stomach as a lion devours the entrails of a wildebeest. It's a topsy-turvy world, where footsteps are created using your hands, wings by flapping a tea towel, and fantastic bone-breaks by twisting celery stalks. The skills of the Foley artist are much-coveted and their methods are frequently hidden from the client, who might not believe that the sounds are created using half the contents of a salad bowl! At these sessions the creation of sounds for surreal inorganic contributions can be fashioned by the treated human voice. And all of this is done in real time while performing synchronously with the pictures on screen.

At the premix the layers are built up progressively, bearing in mind that there will be music and narration to blend in as well. As we now have virtually unlimited tracks, frequently the music will be delivered as 5.1 stems, and sometimes even as orchestral sections with strings, woodwind, percussion etc that can add up to thirty tracks or so just for one piece of music. But that does give you the option to favour one section of the orchestra while maintaining the other sections at a steady level.

At the final mix all this will be blended and balanced with our value-added contribution to suit our clients' tastes. And then the work starts on all the other versions for the other co-producers ...

Distributor

Essentially the role of the distributor is to find markets for a film. This does not just mean finding a broadcaster – it may also involve DVD/BD sales and other products. Films can also be broadcast in many different countries and be repackaged ('versioned') in different ways and in different languages.

Increasingly distributors are not just acquiring (ie signing distribution contracts with) completed films, but are getting involved in the production side. Once distributors have a relationship with broadcasters and other markets, they get to know what is required and will be more likely to be able to provide this if they can steer the production in that direction from the start. That's why you will quite often see the name of a distributor as an executive producer.

Most independent producers will want to know where their film will end up before they start spending money on it, and so will be seeking a distribution deal early on. The distributor will then guide the producer, perhaps even supplying staff, to ensure the result can feed the available markets.

Carl Hall
CEO
Parthenon Media Group

As CEO I lead a highly experienced management team who control the creative, technical, financial and commercial direction of Parthenon Media Group. We have radically grown the business, both organically and through strategic acquisitions, to make it one of the UK's leading independent TV media groups. During my time in the wildlife film industry, I have produced and executive-produced more than 600 hours of programming for global audiences and secured sales and output deals worldwide.

It all started for me over thirty years ago in the post-production office of the legendary *Survival* series at Anglia TV. I bought equipment and supplied technical back-up to some of the true industry greats, like Dieter Plage, Alan Root and Des Bartlett. I went on to train as a cameraman at Anglia, and then moved on to become Technical Director at the Jim Henson Group. I then joined Hit Entertainment as MD of Hit Wildlife and, in 2002, launched Parthenon Entertainment.

The industry has certainly changed a lot over the past ten years, most notably in the technical advances of equipment which have made the previously-unfilmable filmable, and now in HD! It has also been an age of 'adapt and survive' for wildlife programming, as budgets have been squeezed and the genuine wilderness areas have become more and more compromised.

Add to this the 'terms of trade' agreement introduced in the UK in 2007, which gave the rights back to the producer, but meant an end to fully-commissioned programmes for many of them too. This made production companies very aware of the need to exploit their rights fully, to help finance further productions. Many chose distributors, like Parthenon, to secure maximum sales for their content with broadcasters across the globe.

As a direct result the rise of co-production funding for some of the high-quality blue-chip wildlife programming, for which Parthenon is renowned, has had a significant effect on the industry. Few programmes now enjoy the security and freedom of being fully-funded by one broadcaster. The bespoke nature of programming, however, means that for each programme made – often funded by up to four broadcasters – several versions have to be created to look as if the programme was created specifically for each.

In addition the growth of global broadcasters like Discovery, National Geographic and Smithsonian, as well as the proliferation of themed channels such as Nat Geo Wild and Animal Planet, has meant the demand for content has reached levels unheard of ten years ago. Yet it is critical that, though this huge amount of content available 24-hours-a-day, standards are kept high and the quest for truly great images of our beautiful wildlife are paramount.

As for the future, I predict that wildlife programming will need to attract attention across a range of devices and platforms. TV is likely to be controlled via online portals, such as Google, and programmes will be showcased online. These programmes will be enhanced via social media platforms and online fan sites, all profiling product-related merchandise and downloadable 'extras' to help build the series brand online. The rise of 'download to own' and 'video on demand' could also result in the end of linear TV.

For anyone looking to enter the wildlife film industry, it can be a daunting prospect. I would recommend they try to get as wide a range of experiences and disciplines as possible, as this will help them appreciate better what everyone does. Work with the production and distribution teams of companies in the industry, and understand better what broadcasters want, so you can focus your efforts on what works rather than what doesn't. You don't have to rely solely on production companies either. Working with charities, screen agencies and voluntary organisations in wildlife also builds contacts and networking opportunities that can help set you up and build your career for life.

John Watts
Director of Sales & Acquisitions (Distributor)
Octapixx Worldwide

I started in the television broadcast and entertainment industry as a member of the program scheduling team at Discovery Networks Europe, the international satellite broadcaster in the United Kingdom. From there I was able to work as a continuity producer, and eventually progressed to the programming team of Animal Planet International, working on commissions, co-productions and acquisitions. The numerous roles I held within the company allowed me to gain valuable insight into the wide variety of components and departmental functions that comprise an international broadcaster. Working now as a distributor at Octapixx Worldwide, these previous experiences at the broadcast level have proven to be invaluable.

The primary role of the distributor in our industry is to market and deliver content from the producers they represent to international broadcasters and DVD/home video sub-distributors. Increasingly there are digital participants – Netflix among others – who are aggregating content in the digital space. These companies are becoming increasingly important players, and the variety of ways in which consumers can enjoy content is increasing almost daily. Simultaneously new technology has made it cheaper than ever to produce content, resulting in many more producers' trying to market their programmes. In this fragmented environment – where there is a saturation of sellers, and multiple media rights that can be carved out from any one project – the distributor is a valuable partner to producers looking to reach the market, and buyers looking for content from a trusted industry source.

With an ongoing technological shift in the way individuals are consuming content, television broadcasters are regularly expanding the rights they acquire in order to provide their viewers with different options regarding how and when they can enjoy their programming. Among these rights are simulcast streaming, as well as providing online catch-up 'windows' that can be as brief as seven days and as long as thirty, providing the broadcasters with the right to house the program directly on their websites. Presently these rights are regarded as a complement to traditional broadcast rights, but they also have the effect of insulating the broadcaster's business from the onset of on-demand internet and broadcast video services, which provide viewers the opportunity to watch content from wherever and whenever they want. It is the distributor who draws the line as to which rights should be complementary to broadcast and which rights should be segmented elsewhere, all the while prioritising the maximisation of revenue that returns to the producer.

It is vital for international distributors to have an understanding of the programming needs of content buyers in the global marketplace. Being in regular contact with content buyers, Octapixx Worldwide is constantly updated, and advised of their needs and requirements, from creative and technical standpoints. Just as the manner in which broadcasters are delivering content to consumers is changing, so too is the manner in which broadcasters require that content be delivered to them after they have licensed it. The distributor must stay on top of all of these considerations.

Octapixx shares with its producers the content, technological and delivery knowledge that it extracts from the marketplace. As 3D and other new technologies become positioned for increasing relevance to

113

consumers, Octapixx also works with major laboratories and technology providers, better to understand the implications for the producer and for the content buyer.

Distributors are vital to the entertainment industry. There is such complexity at the production level and at the broadcast/home video/DVD/digital level, an intermediary between the two only serves to enhance communication in all directions. We build relationships across the marketplace, and we create demand among buyers for the content created by our producer partners. We are the first to identify new trends in entertainment consumption, and we are the first to identify emerging business models. We are the front line that helps the buyers identify what they want. And we provide the intelligence that helps producers identify what the marketplace needs.

Commissioning Editor

The commissioning editors are the all-important people who decide which films will be broadcast. They will either buy the rights to an already-completed film, or, like some distributors, be involved in the production and style development of the film. They don't just see what films are around, but actively seek programme ideas. They have strict budgets and timescales.

Commissioning editors need to be in touch with what the viewing public wants, and keep abreast of ratings figures and what other channels are doing, predict future trends etc. They are typically inundated by pitches, and a good deal of their time is spent sifting through film proposals looking for ideas that will be right for their network.

Henrik Ekman
Acquisitions Executive - Science and Nature
SVT Sweden

Eken – in i döden levande (*The Oak – Dead and Alive*) – in production)
Wired Wolf
Of Moose and Men

Is there life?

There is one luring trap for both buyers and producers of wildlife films: we all too often assume that the viewers share our passion. Most likely they don't.

I am responsible for buying science and natural history programmes for Swedish Television, SVT. For many years I have also been reporting on nature and the environment as a TV reporter, and have also produced a couple of documentaries. On the wall of my study is a press-cutting from our leading morning daily newspaper, *Dagens Nyheter*, to help me avoid the trap. One of their TV critics declares his lack of interest in wildlife. He prefers to spend his time in the garden with a drink and a cigarette. He has tried, he assures us: wearing the right clothes he has fought his way through dense spruce woods, gazed at magnificent landscapes and faked awe when spotting a red fox. But his heart was never there. It longed for his cultivated garden.

Over the years some of our hosted wildlife shows managed to touch his heart. Perhaps there was some dormant wild heritage there after all. So he sat down with quite high expectations when we started airing the BBC landmark series *Life*, the first episode announced as 'a magic hour'. And he admits the images were amazing: animals moving in extreme slow-motion, flowers blooming in seconds, seeds sailing by in the air and slowly coming to rest in a place just perfect for growth.

He gives *Life* credit for showing us the wonders of nature: how a pine tree can keep growing for five thousand years despite harsh conditions, or how a pygmy gecko clings on to life despite being so small that a single raindrop can knock it off its leaf: 'It is HD sharpness, microscopes, time-lapses, 5.1 Dolby sound and a reverential narration. And it is totally dead. Sterilised.'

Of course I was provoked, having bought the series for SVT. But I read his words with care and they make me think hard about the future of the business. For decades the big producers could rely on technological wonders. The audience was stunned by the beauty and wonders of *Planet Earth*'s imagery, and rightly so. And this development still goes on further and further, into 3D and so on, into perpetuity and beyond ... .

Along the way we run the risk of losing the core element – the story. The powerful TV critic at *Dagens Nyheter* watches *Life* with all its technical achievements and he is bored. It has no ... life.

So what does this tell us about future wildlife film-making?

That there can be, and will be, at least two parallel tracks. The major players will continue producing fascinating blue-chip series with ever more fascinating technology. And I will of course buy them. But along with that there will be a market for wildlife films with a strong story. It may be an environmental message or just the gripping fate of some animal. Good drama is both universal and eternal. It will always have its place, 3D or not.

For a while I feared that the technical demands from us broadcasters would put an end to the promising development brought about by the digital era, with cheap cameras of high quality. Even the smallest independent producer would need to invest big money in HD cameras. But now it seems we've already reached the point where they are affordable.

My feeling is that the genre 'people and nature' will grow stronger. One sign is the major BBC undertaking with the landmark series *Human Planet* (which I of course bought). Films about different cultures with one thing in common: they live off the land and harvest the resources without depleting them. Of course there is wildlife in between, but still much less than you would expect from a series from the BBC Natural History Unit.

The series is a worthy ancestor of *Wild China*, the production where the NHU people realised that increasingly, in some parts of the world, you can't tell stories about nature without including humans. *Wild China* was a great success all over the world including Sweden.

This means that there is room for producers with a knowledge that expands beyond just the behaviour of big cats or sharks. Those charismatic species will continue to capture an audience, but as the population on this planet keeps growing, stories about us and the natural world and how we can co-exist will certainly have a market. The era when all cameramen tried to avoid getting people in the picture in Africa or elsewhere is over.

Of course I may be influenced by the fact that I have a background as a journalist in news media, but that in combination with a degree in biology has given me a good basis for telling stories about wildlife and people. I think quite a few producers will have that combination in the future.

Today my professional role is mainly that of a buyer, with some opportunities to enter projects as a co-producer. I still want to buy the latest BBC series, simply because they are top quality. But just like the negative TV critic longing for his garden, I can sometimes get a bit bored by perfection, and yearn for more personal story-telling, and films that show us – in an interesting way – the familiar nature we have next-door.

A good recent example is *Wild Places of Essex*. Another one I liked very much was *Berlin Beasts*, about all the wild boar and red foxes that have made the German capital their home. No time-lapse, no Heligimbal, just endless hours waiting in the night to get the right shots. The result was surprising and truly entertaining, a film people talked about afterwards. [The Cineflex **Heligimbal** is a recently developed form of gimbal technology in the form of a motion-stabilized helicopter mount for motion picture cameras].

So when I look for new wildlife films for SVT I will go for two things, both the blue-chips and the personal documentaries.

Most importantly, there must be *life*. And why not a sense of humour?

117

Steve Greenwood
Series Editor – *Natural World*
BBC Natural History Unit

Lost Land of the Volcano
Lost Land of the Jaguar
Expedition Borneo

I work at the BBC Natural History Unit, which has been based in Bristol ever since it was first set up over fifty years ago. My current job is as Series Editor of *Natural World*, which is the BBC's only strand of single wildlife documentaries. It has been running for over twenty-eight years now, so it has a long heritage – though, like all television, it is rapidly evolving with the times.

I'm part of a small Natural World team, and we work together very closely on all aspects of the strand. My job has three sides to it. First, it is finding and developing the ideas for the strand. Sometimes they come from inside the NHU, sometimes from independent companies, and sometimes from freelancers. It's rare that the ideas come fully formed, so we invest a lot of time working with the producer in order that the film really stands up, and we know it can be made into a cracking programme.

Second, it is working closely with the producers of the commissioned films throughout the production and post-production phases. Half the films we make are 'in house' and half from independent companies – often local ones. Making films is always an endurance event and full of unexpected pitfalls and curveballs. Sometimes the journey just to reach the edit room with a box of rushes feels like running a marathon. And then the producer has to put the film together – which feels like running another one!

The final part of my job is working with the Natural World team to keep the overall strand fit and healthy and thriving. We have developed strong links with our international co-producers and we put a lot of effort into ensuring everybody is getting the films they need. We also

118

work closely with the BBC2 Controller and her team so that our strand feels fresh and relevant for our audience, and is right for the channel. We have between ten and fourteen films per year, and at least two years of films in some stage of production, so it's a juggling act with many balls in the air.

How did I get into wildlife film-making? I've always loved biology and studied it at university. I also loved filmmaking – though in the 1970s, when I was growing up, I had to borrow my friend's 8mm camera and edit with sticky tape. I have always loved telling people stories about wildlife and wanted to work on the boundaries of wildlife and the media – but after I graduated I found it very hard to find a way in. I tried to get work as a print journalist but there weren't many jobs around – especially for someone with a biology degree. I had various job interviews for the BBC, but they were massively competitive and I wasn't chosen, so I started working on my other love – as a research ecologist. But I kept on writing articles for papers and sending in ideas for radio programmes. Eight years later I was working as an entomologist in the Solomon Islands when I saw an advert in an old UK science magazine saying that the BBC was looking for a scientist to be trained as a radio producer. I think they were so shocked to get a letter from the other side of the world that I managed to blag the job.

The last ten years have seen a revolution in the industry. Cameras and edit gear used to be out of most people's reach, but now anyone can shoot and cut a film; and of course with the web there are many platforms to show it as well. It is on the web where the really exciting changes are going to happen over the next decade. As televisions and computers gradually merge there will also be many new opportunities for getting an audience for the films.

As the Natural History Unit is part of the BBC we have a public service remit – to entertain, educate and inform our audience about the wildlife of the world. With so many new channels and so many new types of factual output to tempt our audiences, the competition is getting tougher. But I think that is good, and we're responding by developing new ideas and types of programmes to excite our audiences about the wonders of the natural world.

However rapidly the digital world changes, there are key skills that underpin it. Being able to tell stories that captivate and enchant an audience is an ancient human skill – and my guess is that we'll need it for many thousands of years to come. Being able to sort through mounds of competing ideas and conflicting information and still telling the story fairly and honestly is also a core skill, whatever the medium. Watching lots of TV and films, and developing a critical eye and ear for what works and what doesn't, is also a great skill to learn.

We are all aware that our job has never been more important. We see the rapid changes happening globally to the natural world and it is all too apparent that so much of its wild beauty and diversity is disappearing. I do believe that finding new ways of engaging people with wildlife and the challenges it faces is a key weapon in forging a more optimistic future. Film-making has a vital role to play.

People often ask me how to get into wildlife broadcasting. My advice is to gain whatever experience you can, wherever you can. It may be in print or in radio or online, and it may be in wildlife films or in other areas. And most importantly, keep knocking on those doors – if you really want it, eventually one will open for you.

Georgina Eyre
Head of Acquisitions
Off the Fence

My current role is as Head of Acquisitions at distribution and production company Off the Fence. I acquire and account-manage all the third-party content we represent and sell on behalf of our independent producers. I work across all factual genres: natural history, science, history, culture, travel, adventure and lifestyle.

I started out in the BBC NHU working as the PA to the Commercial Director, which also included being the overall office manager and initial point person for anyone ringing the unit. The job was never dull. I then went to work with Neil Nightingale at *The Natural World* as his PA and was lucky to work with some terrific producers and on some fantastic productions. From the NHU I went to work in the BBC Commercial

Agency, a department set up to produce distribution and co-production revenue for BBC programmes. I did this for a number of years before heading into the independent world, first as a TV rights consultant and then working for Target Entertainment and Off the Fence in my current capacity in Acquisitions.

The industry has revolutionised itself since I started fourteen years ago. Technology has moved on apace, film being replaced by tape, SD by HD, CGI becoming commonplace in shows, and now the onset of 3D in the documentary landscape. In the distribution world we are working with myriad different platforms: in particular, mobile and internet, and new niche channels are cropping up all the time. This brings the inevitable challenge of managing and selling all these different rights, and OTF has become adept at windowing so that we can maximise revenue from these platforms. Changes will also continue apace as audiences want to view content in different ways, and this will have a knock-on effect on producers and the models they use to fund their programmes.

I envisage that co-productions will continue to work in the wildlife genre but also that the marketplace will become even more competitive for such funding. Producers will also need to look at new models for raising finance. Natural history production will continue to work in the large 3D graphics-led event pieces for theatres. But I also see it continuing as it is with more appetite for character-led, less blue-chip natural history docs that transmit in a 7pm slot to a family audience. We could also be looking at a future where there is more interactive natural history. Viewers will be able to watch whatever they want, whenever they want, through 'bush-cams' and 'underwater-cams'. The internet will also become a useful place for enthusiasts wanting to post clips of what is happening in their own backyards.

My break started with a five-week work placement at the NHU and I never looked back. Wildlife is an incredibly competitive environment and you need to be prepared to work hard. Grasp every opportunity with both hands and never make enemies on the way up, as you can be sure to meet them coming down! In my role it is hugely important to keep an open mind and to be able to watch and appreciate a variety of programmes, however strange you find the production style or subject matter.

Location Manager/Fixer

Sending film-crews on location overseas can be fraught with difficulties and unexpected complications. The producer's best friend in these situations will be the location manager (often known as a 'fixer' in the business) who has a thorough understanding of the needs of a film-crew, and also of the peculiarities of working in a certain part of the world.

Location managers will be working with the producer (probably long-distance) in the planning stages to organise filming permits, licences, permissions, government liaison, scouting, local research etc. Before the crew arrives the location manager will organise transport, accommodation, equipment hire and resolve customs issues etc.. While the crew is actually filming on location there may be further requirements to co-ordinate such as porters, drivers, cooks, shipping films/tapes/hard drives, equipment repair/replacement, or assisting when crew members are hurt or fall ill.

Janice Beatty
Fixer
African Environments – Tanzania

Stephen Tompkinson's African Balloon Adventure – made for ITV by Tiger Aspect.
Science of Migrations, The Great Migrations Series – National Geographic
BBC *Africa* Series and BBC *Life* Series

Working in Tanzania is hugely challenging, often rewarding ... but also very frustrating! My role as a fixer encompasses every stage of production from the initial enquiry through to the crew getting the shots. I am often contacted early on, during the research / concept stage of a project – at this stage the production team have an idea and rough outline of their film but are looking for a location and the intimate details that will bring it to life. At this stage my role is to suggest locations, to research stories and come up with some interesting ideas. On some occasions I am asked to go on a recce to scout out potential locations or characters.

As the project develops my role morphs into offering more advice and facts about operating in Tanzania: the pitfalls, the opportunities and the idiosyncrasies. As the project firms up I work with the production team to help with planning, scheduling and budgeting, suggesting and booking hotels, advising on the best flights to arrive on and arranging internal flights if necessary.

I am fortunate in that my company – African Environments – has specially designed 4x4 filming vehicles, fully-staffed workshops to adapt and modify them to suit individual needs and fully-staffed mobile camps to accommodate crews as they work and film in remote areas.

As the filming date approaches I work closely with the production team and apply for the various government permits and myriad permissions needed. Once I have the equipment lists in hand I will facilitate the import and safe arrival of equipment. On arrival crews spend some time checking and testing their equipment and fitting it into the filming vehicles before heading off into the wild bush!

Once filming starts my role usually becomes one of support, except with more complex shoots involving more interaction with officialdom and local communities when I may go along to co-ordinate. On a purely wildlife-based film within the parks my experienced filming driver guide ensures that the  permits, various fee payments, camp and vehicles are running seamlessly.

During the shoot I will ensure that all the logistics go smoothly, assisting with any issues or the coming and going of crew members and equipment. As the shoot draws to a close – a shoot can be anywhere from a couple of days to six weeks – I will set up the export of their equipment and ensure the crew get off ok.

I have been a Tanzanian resident working with film crews since 1992. I started out as Production Manager with Baron Hugo van Lawick, working with both Partridge Films and Nature Conservation Films. Hugo had a career that spanned over forty years – starting out in Gombe Stream National Park documenting chimpanzees and then moving on to the Serengeti. He had a permanent camp at Ndutu in the south of the Park and from here he and his protégée film-makers forayed into the park to document and film the endless array of wildlife on the rolling plains. My role was to manage the production office in Arusha – the main town in the region. This entailed everything from finance, to keeping the thirty people living in the bush supplied with everything from drinking water to fuel and food as well as overseeing vehicle repairs and the export of film rushes.

On Hugo's retirement (in 1998) I decided to carry on the love affair with film-making and to become a freelance film fixer working through my company African Environments.

One of the main things I have noticed in filming over the past decade has been that filming has not been exempt from the worldwide pressure on time and money! Film crews have less and less time in the field but are still expected to capture even better and more dramatic sequences with less than half the time on location.

The advances in technology, the move to digital has in some ways eased my role – relieving the pressure to get rushes back for developing as fast as possible – but has introduced new aspects such as arranging helicopters with cineflex mounts.

Tanzania has also changed, becoming more popular as a tourist destination; there are more and more regulations to contend with as it becomes more popular. My company has focused on seeking out the wilder places and different angles for film crews – this has meant everything from working on a trans-African hot air balloon odyssey to stalking and filming lions on foot in the Serengeti.

Over the coming decade I can see a divergence in my business. On the one hand is the resurgence of the blue-chip wildlife filming. We have several projects in the pipeline which plan to use cutting-edge technology to bring fresh insights into the intricacies of the vast African ecosystems. On the other hand watching wildlife TV will reveal to everyone the movement towards lower budget / more sensational productions and reality TV. I feel this side of my business will become more of a feature in the years to come.

Over the years my company has invested a lot of time, effort and money into being 'responsible' – this encompasses everything from looking carefully at our footprint and using renewable resources wherever possible – from solar powered camps to charcoal made from waste biomass – right on through to investing in our people through training and mentoring.

Stock Footage Library Manager

Wildlife film-makers, whether large companies or individual independents, will gradually amass large collections of footage not used in their own productions which can be sold as an additional revenue stream. Where large producers are concerned this can mean dealing with thousands of hours of footage. This will be handled by the company's footage library manager(s), or via an independent stock footage library.

One of the aims is to sell sequences to other producers for their productions. For example a film about tigers may be missing an all-important mating scene – if the camera crew have already spent a fruitless year in the jungle then the easiest option is just to purchase this scene from a library and weave it into the film. There are other outlets for footage, though, such as commercials, educational DVDs/BDs, websites, installations and so on.

The library manager will have the task of liaising with customers and locating the footage they require. They will also be responsible for adding new footage to the library and cataloguing it. They will control the viewing of footage by potential customers, either in the studio or over the Internet, and on purchase will negotiate the rights/licenses and fees.

Tom Walmsley
Stock Footage Library Manager / MD
Specialist Stock

Oceans – National Geographic
Whale Wars – Discovery Channel
Natural World – BBC NHU

I started out as a cameraman and photographer (after taking a degree in biology) with a focus on marine life. This was difficult work at the time but meant that I could request copyright of the material I shot. And my travels gave me an opportunity to see most of the world's seas and oceans underwater.

Around the year 2000 to generate a more steady income I set up a stock library for stills and video. A few things I had learnt were still useful:

a) rare or particularly eye-catching material is valuable and deserves concerted and sustained efforts to market it

b) whoever has the best technology in the footage industry (be it cameras or web platforms) will be at an advantage most of the time.

My company, Specialist Stock, currently sells stock (photos and footage) globally to the publishing, broadcast and non-broadcast sectors. We hold a number of branded collections and specialise on the environment through science, society and the natural world.

Since 2000 the main changes to the stock industry have been:

a) a flood of material with a growing range of technical quality, which needs discussing with end users.

126

b) broadcasters demanding a package of rights for the same prices, so there is no room for up-selling; but at least prices are not being eroded as they are with stills sales.

There has been a ground-swell of demand for stock because it is (now) often cheaper than shooting new material. The trend towards interview- or celebrity-led programming lends itself to using stock. However there is no sign of a creamy crest for this wave, first because the interviewees sometimes supply material for nothing and, second because editors can use material sold at very low prices (known as micro-stock) and disguise any technical problems with effects or use it to build CGI.

The most exciting area of the industry is footage research (freelance, for an agency or in a production company). At Specialist Stock we have a Comprehensive Research Facility which charges for research because it is integrated with a global network of suppliers that has taken us fifteen years to build up. The facility means we can find material at low-res relatively quickly for most subject matter (deep archive through lifestyle and wildlife to news). The internet has meant it is possible to view and FTP ['File Transfer Protocol' – ie transfer over the internet] low-res material, followed by the selected high-res clips, to or from any corner of the globe.

Shooting fresh material in the latest format is quite an investment and has risks built in, so it is important to have a unique speciality that helps generate stock sales and multimedia photo-stories (and filming contracts). From a stock researcher's point of the view the number of specialist camera operators who can be accessed around the world now generates an incredible bank of high-quality, interesting shots to draw from.

I would consider carefully what equipment, experience and skills you have to offer the industry and do not rule out freelance work, to start with, in all the sectors mentioned above. Sign up, or get involved with FOCAL International, www.focalint.org (Federation of Commercial Audiovisual Libraries).

'Researchers are the glue of our industry.' **Sue Thexton**, consultant

'Once the majority of library owners have their content available digitally and they join the smart content metadata revolution ... researchers can focus their energy on the insight, creativity and richness of the content they are

working with.' **Kevin Schaff**, CEO and Founder of Thought Equity Motion stock agency (quoted in FOCAL Archive Zones, Summer 2011)

© Tom Walmsley / SpecialistStock

Bottlenose dolphins leaping from waves in Plettenburg Bay, South Africa. The film crew were working with these dolphins which feed in the surf zone. The sand dunes behind show how the waves dump on to the beach from a great height, so fast boats were used to escape the oncoming waves. The pod of dolphins, up to ninety strong, leap simultaneously along the wave at the last possibly opportunity before it breaks, making it dangerous but rewarding work.

Multimedia Producer

Multimedia producers are involved in the many diverse uses wildlife film can be put to, other than television broadcast. They will be involved, for example, in the authoring of products such as websites, interactive installations, portable computer/phone applications and so on. This could involve converting existing wildlife films for use on these new systems, or creating custom-built interactive productions for a variety of applications including education, tourism, product-promotions etc. This may mean collating a vast number of assets such as video, still photographs, text, animations, sound, music, narration etc, and creatively programming them together.

Kim Wolhuter
Producer / Camera Operator
Mavela Media

Stalking Leopards
Predators at War
Hyena Queen / Hyenas at War

"Hey Kim, do you want to join me making wildlife documentaries?" said old-time school-friend Richard Goss on the other end of a phone.

"No not really, why would I want to do something silly like that?" I replied.

My legendary grandfather, Harry Wolhuter, was the first game ranger in the Kruger National Park and my father followed in his footsteps. I had the good fortune of inheriting their passion, and also followed a career in wildlife management. Film-making had never entered my mind.

Richard eventually convinced me and, having worked as an assistant on *The Sisterhood*, he gave me a movie camera, ten rolls of film, and said, "Go for it". I worked as a cameraman with Richard for the following six years and finally stepped into the unknown world of independence, where I've now been lurking successfully for the past seventeen years.

For most of this time I've had the privilege of being able to spend at least eighteen months on productions that followed a pack of hyaenas, a lion pride or a specific leopard, getting to know them intimately. These long shoots allowed the story develop on its own, in its own time.

The beauty of it, too, was that I developed a relationship with wild animals the likes of which I had never imagined. Finding myself sprawled out, chilling and playing with a wild hyaena as if it were a domestic cat or dog, was way beyond what humans can normally do!

For me, just to be accepted and allowed into any wild animal's personal space is an incredible privilege and the ultimate honour. As with my everyday filming in wildest Africa, I have to keep reminding myself not to take it for granted. No film-maker should. It's about the lifestyle, and wildlife film-making allows me to live this amazing wild life.

Now that I was interacting more with my subjects, my career took a slight twist: I'm finding myself in front of, as well as behind, the camera. I don't fancy myself as a presenter; but film me doing what I so passionately love, and I'm happy to share it with the outside world.

Today I still shoot films over extended periods but have more recently found myself caught out, in that budgets over the last five years have been dramatically slashed.

Films are now being shot in four to six weeks and consequently the stories have to be more and more contrived to make the footage work. Around the same time that budgets were being slashed, the talk at film festivals was that the internet was the future for wildlife documentaries. But nobody had the recipe for how this was going to work.

A friend of mine, Chris Boden, already involved in putting media on to mobile systems, suggested we start with a blog, pictures and wildlife podcasts. And so www.wildcast.net hit cyberspace in 2006 – the idea being to offer free content online daily and give people places where they could interact and so help build the community. (YouTube was already doing well, but Facebook had hardly taken off). We hoped that once Wildcast was generating significant traffic we could then monetise the content through advertising and sponsorship on the site.

Every day I religiously put out a blog, photos and an edited three-minute video clip. For three years I kept this going so that today there are over 1,000 podcasts and some 8,000 photos on Wildcast. But it still wasn't monetising itself and the effort, about three hours a day, just wasn't worth it. So what went wrong, or was it doomed from the start?

Wildcast was a first. Others followed with different models, but still today nobody seems to be making a successful go of wildlife on the internet. If I ever started up Wildcast again, I'd probably make the podcasts more 'reality' styled, using myself as a character, and make the clips shorter to hit that 'sweet-spot' of between forty-five and ninety seconds. Facebook and Twitter are now well established and could just help generate that extra needed traffic.

I suppose, as wildlife film-makers today, we have to be grateful there are twenty-four-hour channels hungry for content! Huge amounts of content. But cheap content, unfortunately.

In order for me to continue to live the lifestyle I'm so fond of, I have to find a way of making good shows on a fraction of the original budgets. (Anybody know how? Please help!) At the same I want to be sure to maintain the integrity of the wildlife and appease my father and grandfather.

As 'silly' as it may have seemed (when I responded off-the-cuff to my old-time school-friend) ... I don't believe there is a more fulfilling career in wildlife than that of a wildlife film-maker. You get to make your movie and watch it ... and I get to sleep more hours on a camera box than any other profession does. The media has to be the greatest tool for creating awareness about our natural world. Use it creatively and wisely but don't abuse it.

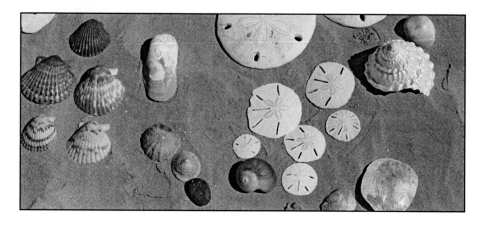

Ben Waddams
Wildlife Artist / Journalist
Freelance

Wild About Art – BBC (producer: Elaine Bancroft)
The One Show (wildlife segment) – BBC/**Tigress Productions**
Austin Stevens Adventures – **Tigress Productions** (producer: Sarah Peat)

I am a natural history journalist and wildlife artist. I have also worked as a researcher and editorial assistant with natural history production companies. I also film and present my own wildlife videos for a web audience. I write for local, county-specific, and national publications on the provincial wildlife that may be found in proximity to my readers throughout the year. In the art world I produce work for individuals, publishers and writers as well as my own shows, demonstrations and exhibitions. I endeavour to consolidate my art and journalism with charity events in an effort to preserve the wildlife I am so fond of.

I grew up on the New England coast of North America where I remember watching one of my first video cassettes, *Life on Earth*: the famous scene of David Attenborough walking along a beach strewn with crawling, breathing (and copulating!) 'living fossils' – horseshoe crabs – was filmed just a few miles from my house. What I was seeing on the screen had been happening outside my back door and I was inspired to find it for myself.

132

A decade or so later I bought my first video camera and combined it with a trip to Africa. There I fell in love with the activity of using field craft to approach wildlife, then film and photograph it, to the extent that I felt compelled to make short films on the local wildlife back home in England. How better to see if I was any good at that, than by broadcasting the films on YouTube for all to watch, enjoy and, I hope, learn from.

Technology has improved so much over the last ten to twenty years. My first camcorder was enormous compared to today's mobile phone-sized cameras, and yet it was still a revolution in its day, allowing me to begin filming wildlife easily and cheaply. Today, cameras are even smaller, easier, cheaper and of better quality. This has meant that absolutely anyone can go out and make their own wildlife films. This is true on a professional level as well as an amateur one, for, as the fragmentation of the televisual audience has increased, there are more opportunities for small production crews (sometimes comprising just two people) to make meaningful films with low budgets. This can of course be a curse as well as a blessing, but in the right hands it is a wonderful prospect for new wildlife film-makers.

Why did I get into wildlife film-making and journalism? I expect the answer is the same for everyone in this book: because we are fascinated and intrigued by the animals and plants that make up this planet. My hopes and expectations are that there will be a new generation of wildlife films and film-makers who are guided and enthused by environmental issues – there surely has to be, for we are losing the species on this planet at an alarming rate. I do not propose that all wildlife films of the future will be on solely environmental themes, but that there be a large contingent of productions that will carry a strong environmental message as well as stunning imagery and original storylines.

Wildlife films can utilise 3D technology, better cameras for clearer pictures, and interactive formats such as the web, to draw in the public in new and wider ways. But on the amateur side of things I expect there also to be a revolution. Politically we are already seeing the power of the internet as an overpowering force in the world through websites such as Facebook and YouTube. All the major television broadcasters offer hours of web material as part of their armoury, and many, such as the Discovery networks, the BBC and ITV, have hundreds of hours of wildlife films stored on the web for public viewing. I'd like to foresee a time when amateur film-makers can create part of their career out of producing quality natural history programmes entirely for a web-based audience and on an international platform. I hope this, in turn, will enthuse even more people to protect the natural world and find their own fascination within it.

For most professions there are a number of ways in. This is true for wildlife film-making and journalism too, but every single one of us had the same driving passion at the start: an interest in wildlife. I have been inspired by many people to explore exotic places and bizarre creatures but my interest in nature is home-grown. I did not try to follow in anyone's footsteps as there was no one I knew doing what I wanted to do fifteen years ago. It was my love and appreciation for the natural world that instigated my passion to communicate its wild characters to others, especially the less appealing ones, such as snakes, scorpions and spiders.

My advice is simple: go out there, grab a camcorder and get stuck in to the wildlife that surrounds you. I have always enjoyed seeking out wild animals both in my own back garden and in the wilder places on the planet, but the additional appendage of a cheap video camera is a delightful bonus and brings me even greater pleasure as an amateur naturalist. If I can use that camera to communicate my own emotions and experiences to others, it serves as a wholly satisfying reinforcement of that pleasure.

Mike Linley
Producer
Hairy Frog Productions

World of Survival
Animals in Action
The Animal Show with Stinky and Jake (The Jim Henson Company)

Non-Broadcast Markets

For over twenty years I was a producer of the well-known ITV wildlife series *Survival*. When it closed in 2001 I set up my own production company, Hairy Frog Productions Ltd, in Norwich. During the first four years I was involved in productions for Granada Wild, Discovery, Animal Planet and National Geographic (Kratz Brothers), but trying to get productions commissioned by the major broadcasters proved difficult and the situation has worsened since.

134

So, what to do? I had bought a Canon XL1 camera in 1999 and used it to supplement shooting on some *Survival* productions such as *Frogs – The Movie*. It was particularly useful for filming frogs at night without the need for generators, redhead lights, long cables, etc. A simple Maglite torch taped to the top of the camera was all that was necessary. I was impressed by the quality, especially when using 35mm stills lenses on it via an adapter. When not employed I went out into the Norfolk countryside with my stills and video cameras and began building up a library. It's very important to log all your stills and video clips so you know what you have and where to find it. To date the stills library stands at 40,000 slides and 80,000 digital images, and the digital video library contains over 1,000 hours of material. Since buying the Canon XL1 I have used the Canon XM2, XL2 and XLH1 (HDV) and more recently the Panasonic AF101 AVCHD camera.

I have sold stills to various clients and video clips to a variety of broadcast productions, which is fine as far as it goes. You can also sell your material online via sites such as iStockphoto (stills) and Pond5 (video), and this, too, can be moderately successful. But I was determined to find an outlet for my material in a more creative and substantial way. I collaborated with Poppyland Publishing to produce three one-hour DVDs on the wildlife of East Anglia that were reasonably successful.

But it was a chance conversation with the Broads Authority (BA) Press Officer at a function on a nature reserve in Norfolk that led to my latest 'production': the Interactive Touchscreen Visual Display. The BA had been promised money from Europe to develop some sort of visual display: the only problem was that their deadline was the end of the year, after which the offer would be retracted and the money refunded to Europe. Could I produce and deliver three interactive display units by Christmas Eve? The date was 13 October – I had just over two months. I of course said 'yes – no problem', as you do!

I knew plenty about wildlife, enough about filming, but little about editing and absolutely nothing about developing software for touchscreen technology. I needed help. Piers Warren agreed to edit the video material from the library and I turned to the only people I thought might know something about touchscreens – Ugly Studios in Norwich.

They were certainly the right people, and we set about outlining what we thought the BA wanted. It comprised an animated home screen, two hundred fact files of Broads species (each with information, thirty-second video clips and three to four stills per species), aerial footage of the Broads, top places to see wildlife of the Broads and habitats of the Broads – oh, and a ten-minute, narrated video about the Broads. All within the framework of a touchscreen where you can move between areas and cross-reference at will.

The Broads Authority liked it!

Here's the project in more detail – just one example of alternative uses for your wildlife footage other than a traditional 'film'.

Anatomy of a Multimedia Production

The Hardware

The screen we eventually decided to use was the Clever LCD Touch Dual 44 inch. It was the right size, sensitivity and tough enough for constant public use – and was full 1080 HD.

The computer (which is housed, with keyboard and mouse, in a cupboard under the screen) was powered by an Intel Core i5 – 650 processor, 3.20 Ghz with 4MB cache, 4 GB DDR3 RAM and ITB SATA II hard drive. The onboard graphics card was fine for what we needed.

The Display

The system is designed so that the visitor centre staff can simply turn it on in the morning and off in the evening, leaving it to run all day without attention. The permanent stand-by screen is a two-minute video loop of the Broads: aerials, scenics, wildlife and flowers designed to attract the attention of the user. Across it is a banner: 'Broads Wildlife Touchscreen – press to explore'.

Broads Wildlife Touchscreen - press to explore

Once touched this takes you to the 'Home' screen, which offers the user five options:

- Broads wildlife explorer
- About the Broads video
- Top wildlife Sites
- From the air
- Broads habitats

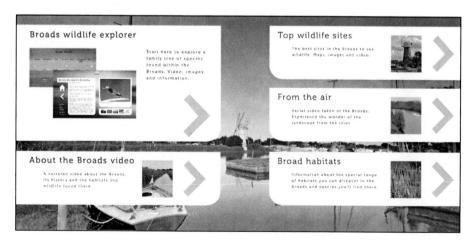

Touching any of these tabs takes you through to that area. You are then offered a 'Family Tree' with branches entitled Amphibians, Birds, Fish, Flora, Invertebrates, Mammals and Reptiles, each with a thumbnail image.

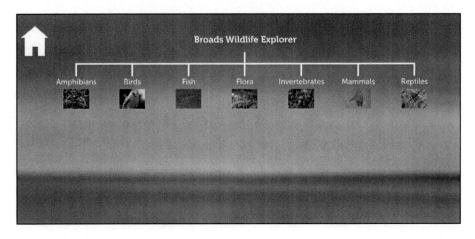

Touching the branch or image takes you further up the family tree. On the left-hand side of the screen is a white 'house' icon that will instantly take you back to the Home page. A backwards-pointing arrow simply takes you back one step.

A short family tree branch, such as Amphibians,

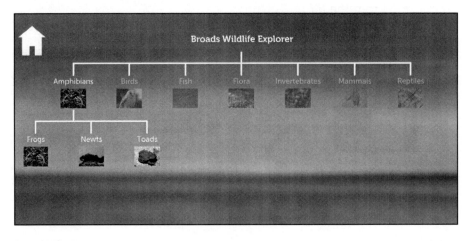

has a small number of further branches – Frogs, Newts and Toads – which then take you to specific species.

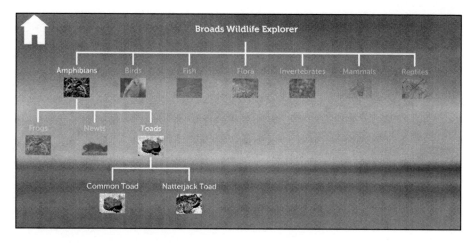

Long family tree branches, such as Birds or Invertebrates,

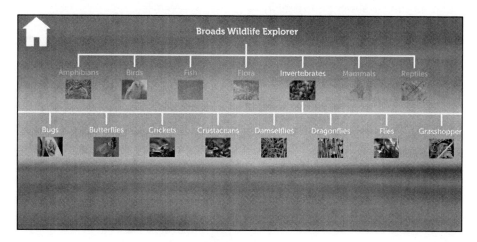

offer you a much larger number of icons and you have to drag your finger across the screen to the left or right to scroll through the options.

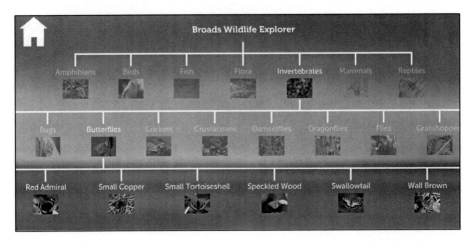

Either way the screen will eventually take you to a single species file such as the Swallowtail butterfly.

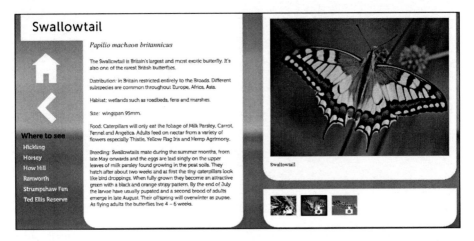

The onscreen information includes scientific name, description, distribution, habitat, size, food and breeding. There is also a thumbnail for a thirty-second video clip of the species, and icons for still images, one of which is already occupying the 'image' box. On the left-hand side of the screen is a 'Where to see' list of the best places to find this species. From this Fact File page you can either go back to the home page, go back one stage and explore other butterflies, or touch one of the places listed in the 'Where to see' list, which will immediately take you to the Fact File for that location.

You are now in the 'Top wildlife sites' section of the display (which you could also access via the Home page). There you will find images of the reserve, a location map and information about facilities and what species to look out for while visiting the location.

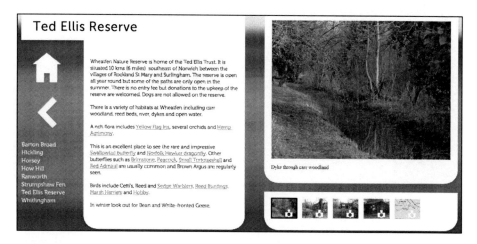

If any of the species listed are underlined and highlighted in blue it means there is a fact file on that species: touching its name will take you directly to that specific fact file. Again from this 'Top wildlife site' page you can go back one stage, return to the Home page, or choose another top location from the offered list. If you navigate to the 'Top wildlife sites' Home page

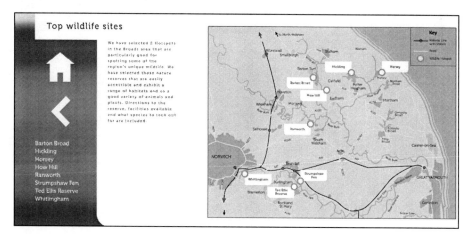

there is a map of the Broads area showing the listed reserves: on touching any, you will be offered a fact file for that location.

From the main Home page you can choose to select the 'From the air' option.

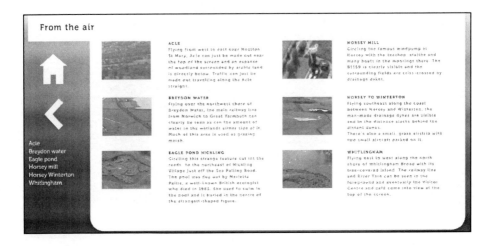

From here you can watch any of six video clips of various parts of the Broads area as seen from the air. You could also select the 'Broads habitats' tab

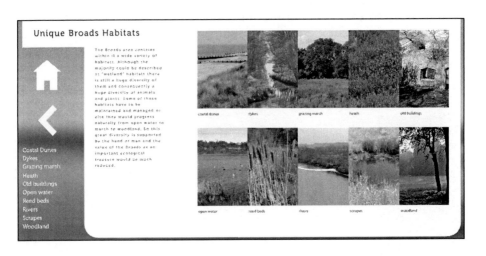

on the Home page and this will give the option of exploring ten different habitats found in the Broads area. For each habitat there is a video clip, several still images and information.

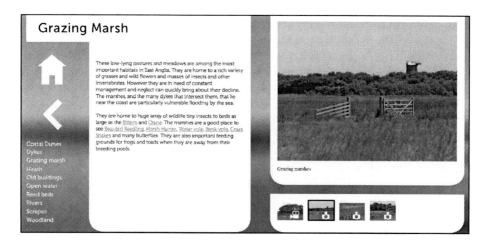

Again by touching any of the species mentioned in the information that is underlined and highlighted in blue you can navigate directly to the fact file for that species.

The final tab on the main Home page is a link to the ten-minute video about the Broads that has music and narration.

Ten minutes, it was decided, is probably the maximum time anyone would stand and watch a screen in a visitor centre, especially when yours truly has done the voice-over!

If the screen is left, or not touched, for two minutes (except over the video) it reverts to the two-minute video loop and plays it until the screen is touched again.

To date the screens have proven to be very popular with adults and children alike. We are now modifying the software and changing some of the content to produce screens that can be tailored for 'Wildlife of Suffolk' or 'Wildlife of Devon', etc., in fact anywhere in the UK. These will involve some local shooting before completion but the vast majority of the stills and video clips are already on file in the library. The Broads touchscreen uses approximately 130 minutes of video, 800 stills, 240 specially-written fact files and about 20 specially created graphics. In all it occupies about 38Gb on the hard drive. It's simple to update by altering the texts and any number of species fact files can be added: their relevant thumbnails will appear on the family tree in the Broads Wildlife Explorer.

In conclusion

It would be too time-consuming and expensive to shoot the required material specially for a project like this – it's important you build up an extensive, well-organised library.

Like most people in the industry I use Apple Mac computers for video and stills storage and manipulation – BUT the touchscreen running software (which uses Flash) is developed on a PC so there is a lot of conversion of material going on.

You can use SD material if it's going to be played in the viewer within each fact file, but anything played full screen has to be shot in HD to maintain quality.

We are now looking at developing similar products for iPhone, iPads etc, and for Smart touchscreens used in schools. It may not be broadcasting as we know it, but in the rapidly-changing world of media this is a good example of a way of using your wildlife images to educate, entertain and reach new audiences.

The Interactive Touchscreen Visual Display in action

3D Producer

The role of the 3D producer is essentially the same as traditional producers with all the extra complexities that working in 3D involves! These generally include larger technical crews, more and heavier equipment, logistical implications, bigger budgets and a great deal of planning in advance of any shoot.

Phil Streather
CEO
Principal Large Format (PLF)

Producer and corporate credits on
Bugs! 3D (for IMAX screens 2003)
Carmen in 3D (for 3D Digital Cinema, RealD and Royal Opera House 2011)
Meerkats 3D (OSF in association with PLF for 3DTV, Sky 3D National Geographic Channels 2011)
Madama Butterfly 3D (for 3D Digital Cinema, RealD and Royal Opera House 2012)

I am a 3D producer, currently working between the genres of natural history and filmed live events such as opera. My most recent films at the time of writing are *Meerkats 3D*, produced by Oxford Scientific Films in association with PLF for National Geographic Channels/Sky 3D and *Madama Butterfly 3D* from the Royal Opera House (presented by RealD and Royal Opera House), directed by Julian Napier. I also run training programmes, including the 2011 National 3D Training Programme funded by Skillset and Sky (www.advanced3d.co.uk).

I got started in 3D through the IMAX business. In 1998 and 2000 I produced two IMAX 2D movies; but IMAX was going 3D. All the films making money were in 3D; at any one time seven or so of the top-grossing IMAX films were 3D. So, through my company PLF, I first presented *Bugs! in 3D* to the IMAX world in 1999. The film, which went into distribution in 2003 with SK Films Toronto, was directed by Mike Slee and narrated by Judi Dench. *Bugs!* has grossed over $40m at the global box office and won many awards, including the prestigious Panda Award for Best Large Format Film at the Bristol Wildscreen Film Festival in 2004 and the Best Special Venue Program Award at Jackson Hole 2009 for the Digital twenty-five-minute version. Before all the IMAX fun I was a sound recordist (eg *The Ark* with Molly Dineen) and before that an offline editor for documentaries.

After the success of *Bugs!* I thought further IMAX 3D films would flow thick and fast, but they are very expensive and difficult to get off the ground; I stuck at it but 2004 to 2007 were lean years for me and 3D. I got by on development budgets and savings!

Then a paradigm shift happened. Digital cameras and digital projection had got good enough and small enough for 3D to emerge from IMAX theatres and public-attraction venues into mainstream cinema. Hollywood saw the dollar signs and big names from Katzenberg to Cameron were on board, seeing the 3D future. I was back! While Cameron was in a massive production schedule on *Avatar* others were getting on with it and *U23D* from 3ality Digital in 2007 proved live action 3D was viable. At the same time I managed the post-production transition of *Bugs!* from IMAX 3D to 3D Digital Cinema, which gave me great insight into the mechanics of 3D. The most important thing I learned, as cowboy 3D operations were springing up everywhere in the UK, was that for good 3D you had to do more than place two broadcast cameras side by side. *Bugs!* had used distances between the cameras (interaxial) as small as 5mm and as large as 5m, and for a reason: that is what it takes to do great 3D. It is a big myth that the optimum distance between the cameras for good 3D is eye-width. So, in 2008, I decided to get even more hands-on and bought the UK's first P+S Technik 3D mirror rig for HD capture, and with Pablo Post produced elements of the 2008 Sky 3D TV tests, particularly *Gladiators*. At that point I realised my 3D future was forever digital and not film. A good break came in 2009 and, in association with Centre Screen Productions of Manchester, I produced the groundbreaking 3D film for the Merlin Entertainments London Eye 4D Experience. The director was my mate Julian Napier.

Since then Julian and I have been fortunate to work together on further large-scale projects. In 2010 I produced, and Julian directed, *Carmen in 3D* from the Royal Opera House (presented by RealD and Royal Opera

147

House). Then in 2011 I produced, and Julian directed, *Madama Butterfly 3D,* also from the Royal Opera House, and once more presented by RealD and Royal Opera House.

So, that's me up to date in 2011. The future is a tough one to call! The two big things to look out for (or to see if they have come to pass!) are: autostereoscopic TV (3D without glasses) and Light Field cameras. Some say until the glasses disappear then 3DTV in the home will not reach its potential. Maybe. My personal opinion is that once the majority of 3DTVs use the same passive glasses that are used in cinemas (such as RealDs) then 3DTV will settle down and be glasses-based for many years to come – say five to ten. Not least because autostereo displays are currently so expensive in order to come anywhere NEAR the quality of current 46"-plus 3DTVs. Others, particularly set manufacturers, are more positive! As to whether Light Field cameras come to dominate 3D production, to be honest I don't understand the science: I just know some people think they are the future – just Google 'Lytro' and 'Light Field cameras' once a year and see where it leads you!

Below are my **Ten Top Tips for Natural History 3D**. Descriptions of TV channels, movies, cameras and rigs used in 3D are all 'at the time of writing', in this case 2011. Over time all will be superseded.

1. Story: any film, whether it is 2D or 3D, starts with story. 3D does not make a bad film better, only a good film different.

2. Read and learn: it's important to decide what type of 3D you like. The best place to start is by watching and reading and reading and watching. There are some great books out there. As of 2011 the best are: Bernard Mendiburu's two books: *3D Movie Making: Stereoscopic Digital Cinema from Script to Screen* and *3D TV and 3D Cinema: Tools and Processes for Creative Stereoscopy,* and Ray Zone's book: *3-D Filmmakers: Conversations with Creators of Stereoscopic Motion Pictures.*

3. Watch and learn: Sky 3D launched in October 2010 in the UK. As of 2011 there are dozens of 3D channels around the world – an outlet for 3D content only dreamed-of ten years ago. If you are serious about getting into 3D then you must buy a 3D TV and watch as much as you can. 3D Blu-rays are also available and every week another 3D feature opens. Watch them all –in the cinema and on a 3D TV. Get a ruler out and measure the difference (parallax) between the images on your 3D TV. Think in terms of pixels or percentages of parallax. Work out which is the left and right eye. Is stuff coming out of the screen at all (negative parallax) or is it all behind the screen (positive)? How much negative parallax do you like? Find out if it is native 3D or converted 3D. Decide what you like about 3D and ask questions of those who know more than you about how the 3D you like was created.

4. Training: the best training courses are the ones where there is plenty of good 3D equipment on hand, and qualified trainers to show you what to do with it. Sony run such courses in LA at the Sony 3D Technology Centre; such courses in the UK are run by the BBC Academy (www.bbcacademy.com) and by me (www.advanced3d.co.uk). There are others too of course! One of the best things about going on courses is that you meet potential collaborators, all fired-up about the potential of 3D to enhance storytelling. After your training buy a GoPro 3D camera set-up, which includes basic 3D-editing software, and get shooting and editing and watching your own stuff.

5. 3D Rigs: some 3D can be shot with the cameras side by side (back of the hall/top of the stadium for live, time lapse in the great out doors with closest object in the distance). BUT, most 3D needs a mirror rig if full-size cameras are used. This is so that the distance between the centres of the lenses (interaxial) can be small enough for the 3D to work properly.

6. Lenses: one of the key things that will become apparent on training courses, or testing, is that the lens that might be best for 2D natural history storytelling (the long lens) will not be your friend in 3D. A 300m lens will result in images that appear as cardboard cut-outs; so will a 100mm lens for that matter, unless your subject is very close to its background and you can increase the interaxial without that resulting in too much 3D in the background. 3D is at its most rounded and lifelike (if that is what you are after!) when you use a relatively wide-angled lens. In 35mm terms, 24mm (Epic/Alexa/Phantom 65) and then 9.7mm in 2/3" chip video cameras are optimum. Beyond 80mm/32mm you will lose the internal 3D coherence of the piece and head into cardboard cut-out territory, unless, as stated above, your subject is very close to its background.

7. Subject matter: if you want the 3D to look rounded and lifelike then you need subjects that are large that you can get reasonably close to (say elephants) or small that you can get pretty close to (say meerkats) or very small that you can get as close to as you like (say insects and plants).

149

8. Dingle: in natural history shooting it is often the case that the subject (particularly in long grasses, woods, rainforest etc.) is partly framed by 'dingle' (foliage etc). In 3D you have to be careful on this one. If the dingle is pretty close to the subject you can get away with it. The dingle will be in negative parallax (in front of the screen) but should be manageable, say 2% negative. But if the dingle is too close to the camera, even if very out-of-focus, you will either have to dial down the 3D (by reducing the interaxial to the point where the shot looks pretty much 2D), cut the dingle down or reframe the shot. If you don't do one of these three things the dingle will have a huge and distracting negative parallax, say 5–10%.

9. Time lapse: time lapse looks great in 2D and fantastic in 3D; DSLRs are perfect for this job as the picture quality is better than most digital video cameras and they are relatively cheap. Use the same approach as live action. The only disadvantage of DSLRs is that when side-by-side the interaxial is about six inches. So, only shoot with cameras side-by-side if the closest object is about twenty feet away. Otherwise use a mirror rig. If you want some fun then put the cameras twenty-five feet apart and make clouds look magical and voluminous (nearest objects hundreds of feet away, mind you!).

10. Negative Parallax: don't be afraid to use negative space. 1% negative is the great unexplored territory of 3D storytelling. Go there and you find trailblazers like Phil McNally (Stereoscopic Supervisor DreamWorks) and Julian Napier (*London Eye 4D*, *Carmen in 3D* and *Madama Butterfly 3D*) – I will also be lurking in the bushes!

Mike Slee
Writer / Director / Producer
3D Specialist

Meerkat Manor – The Story Begins.
BUGS! 3D – A Rainforest Adventure.
Among the Apes – Mountain Gorilla, Orangutan

Elephants, eagles, flamingos, turtles, meerkats and mantis, and now the amazing monarch butterfly. Having made wildlife films starring all of the above, and many more of nature's never-ending marvels, if there is one thing I have learnt it is that nothing in the world of natural history film-making is ever a breeze.

I should have clocked this on Day 1 when, as a junior film-editing trainee (tea boy!) on the first-ever David Attenborough masterpiece *Life on Earth*, I was trusted with the task of logging the film negative of the moment a frog spat out the young, incubating in its mouth. A stack of film cans taller than me, months of patience behind a camera, all for 72 frames, three seconds. One of the most amazing moments in thirteen hours of mind-blowing natural history television from a series that broke ground for everything we do today.

I mention this because over thirty-three years later research, dedication and discipline, combined with the knowledge and preparation that went into that moment, are still the key to natural history film-making and always will be. And whether it's shot high speed, macro, 3D or even a hologram, it's nature's diversity and complexity in front of the camera that continues to amaze.

Flight of the Butterflies 3D, the 3D giant screen feature I am currently making, aspires to these kind of moments of pure unadulterated amazement.

151

Flight of the Butterflies is the sibling and the product of the box-office success and awards bonanza that our previous giant screen movie, *Bugs 3D – A Rainforest Adventure*, garnered. It's a kind of sequel, I guess!

The success of *Bugs* prompted cinemas, science foundations and wildlife protection agencies to talk to us about offering more money for more macro marvels from the insect world. Our job as producers was to come up with a proposition to turn these compliments into cash for the next project.

One particular shot in *Bugs* got the audience on their feet and sometimes even standing on their seats! A river valley in Borneo filled with butterflies in glorious 3D fluttering in the sunlight was the shot in question. So, went the thinking, if one shot gets THAT reaction then imagine a whole movie of butterflies doing their thing in 3D on the giant screen – irresistible. Sure, but what's the story?

And so began five years of research, scriptwriting, re-writing, pitching, promises, negotiations, testing, planning, more promises, more re-writes, more testing and promises broken. Each step of the way we were spending as much time working on how to fund the film as on how to find the story and get the shots. One thing's for sure ... however difficult it is getting nature to behave for your camera, it is likely to be more difficult to get those rare, elusive investors to put their hands in their pockets!

So how do natural history feature films get made? Or, in particular, how does a multi-million dollar movie starring a creature the size of a postage stamp, that weighs no more than a flower petal, get made? Good question: the short answer is never give up on a good idea ... but of course there is more to it than that.

As with most movies it's all about the story and what it makes you think. It doesn't have to be much more than stag meets hind, stag loses hind, stag finds hind! But there has to be a driving purpose behind the immaculate imagery so as to engage your audience's brains. To take David Attenborough's *Life on Earth* again, his story was about witnessing and trying to understand the marvels and anomalies of evolution: simple, eh? But done immaculately, it got you thinking and wondering.

Our first 3D feature *Bugs* was about two rainforest insects whose lives intertwined; the story was simple – how will their interaction play out? What this small story revealed was the diversity and complexity of the rainforest and how the very small creatures play the biggest parts.

Flight of the Butterflies 3D is a little more complex. It's about the most unusual insect migration on earth (good start) and the mind-blowing fact that not until 1972 did science figure out where a billion butterflies disappeared to every Fall in North America (great punchline!).

Unusually for blue-chip natural history films (though it's becoming less so) *Flight of the Butterflies* also involves a human journey. It follows one man's fifty-year quest to discover the facts behind one of nature's great mysteries, and intercuts it with the annual cycle of a monarch butterfly and its epic odyssey from Canada to Mexico. So that's the sell – but who would buy it?

Well, the story takes place across three countries: Canada, USA and Mexico. So they were the first port of call for the cash. The US National Science Foundation, after much consultation and reams of supporting material and educational outreach proposals, finally came on board with the key first monies – a large percentage of which will go to support the movie's educational aims.

The first money in is always key ... it's human nature to wait and see if anyone else thinks an idea is worth backing. So be bold and creative in looking for that first commitment.

Next it was to Mexico for me and my fellow producers Jonathan Barker and Phil Streather. Never before had such a large, complex 3D natural history feature been funded in Mexico – so each small step was a mountain to climb. Last ports of call were Canada and the UK, where a large percentage of our production skills were drawn from. Here a combination of tax incentives, private investors and goodwill slowly, but surely, completed the funding.

Eight years from beginning development we had the money (promised) to make another movie. It was extra lengthy because the budget needed to make a complex natural history feature in 3D is over fifty percent more than the 2D equivalent. And that's for good reason ... shooting wildlife in 3D is technically very complicated – even more so than drama or conventional documentary. The reason is that close-ups and long-lens shots, the staple of natural history, are frustratingly the most challenging to make work for 3D.

For us humans seeing in 3D is no big deal: it's what we do, without thinking, every waking hour of our lives – our brain processes 3D imagery to make it work in a simple single stereo image – but it is, in fact, a most complex optical/neural routine that machines can barely manage. So, add the unpredictable nature of nature to the infuriating process of shooting 3D, and you have got a new kind of torture for film-makers!

But it not just a one-way trade. Technology is both the bane and the brother of natural history film-making and, I have to confess, in the eight years between *Bugs 3D* and *Butterflies 3D*, advances in the technology have changed everything.

Perhaps the most significant development is the lightweight digital cameras with post-trigger (the ability to be able to take the shot AFTER the action has happened). Being able to 'roll' high-speed, high definition continuously on to a hard drive, and therefore wait for the moment to happen and store it, has meant a major change in the way the planning of a complex natural behaviour shoot can fit into a schedule and a budget.

Ironically it is not quicker or cheaper: it's just less of a lottery. You still wait for the critter to perform, and of course that time is money, but it's more manageable. Now a skilled team, sent to the right location at the right time, is more likely to get what is needed when it happens. It used to be a case of "I have all the shots for a sequence except the special one" – so another three weeks would go by, and another thirty rolls of stock, to get the one shot that was needed to complete the story. To get this meant the camera must be running at precisely the right time and even the best film-maker can't guarantee that. Today you still need the skill, patience and experience, but the technology of continuous-record gives you that much-needed break – the odds are better that you record the shot.

Oh! ... that is unless you are shooting on 3D! Twice as much to go wrong, twice as much time to set up and half the chance of having both cameras running smoothly in sync at the same time. But again, don't look back. When everything is running smoothly the potential to capture nature's secrets is at your fingertips.

As I sat in the BFI London IMAX on a wet morning in May 2011 and watched on the giant screen the 120 frames-per-second slow motion rushes of millions of monarch butterflies dancing through the forests of Mexico in glorious 3D it all felt worthwhile.

I was truly grateful for the 70ft motion-controlled Techno Crane that thirty Mexican grips carried up to 10,000 feet, and the state-of-the-art stereo Phantom and Epic cameras, and the specialist operators, and the 3D beam-splitter, and the truck-loads of digital magazines that recorded the spectacular beguiling behaviour of a million butterflies in stunning slow motion all in striking 3D. It's great when a plan comes together!

New technologies now abound to help wildlife storytelling: from mini-cams to night-vision, from thermal-imaging to satellites and super-slow motion, to post-trigger, from microscopy to 3D. All offer exciting new ways to observe and share our world.

And that's why it's never been so good to be behind the camera in natural history film-making ... in front it remains, as ever, up to nature's eternal brilliance.

Views from the Industry

In this section we have invited a number of people, all connected with the wildlife film-making industry in some way, to give their views on the changes they have seen in the industry, and the changes they foresee.

In order to give the widest possible selection of views, we have again invited people at different stages of their careers, from different countries, and from different viewpoints. We have wildlife film-festival directors, producers, authors and educators, and from countries as diverse as China, Japan, the UK, the USA, New Zealand and South Africa. Some have had long illustrious careers and can give us the benefit of having seen changes over a number of decades, others are at the beginning of their careers – for we should also take good note of those who are the future of wildlife film-making. For example, we include the winner of the Newcomer category in Wildscreen's 2010 Wildlife Film Festival (Mat Thompson) and a fifteen year-old aspiring film-maker who has yet to start his career but is already taking the right steps (Alex Rhodes).

You will see that some views are controversial and some of the contributors disagree with each other. Some are positive and hopeful for the future, others are frustrated and long for change. One theme common throughout is the passion that people have for this industry. It is unlikely to make you rich (although there have been a few exceptions) and at times you may find yourself spending long periods working for nothing. But once in, most people are 'bitten by the bug' and wouldn't want to do anything else.

After we have heard from all the contributors we draw some conclusions – gathering together common threads and predictions. It will be fascinating to look back in ten years' time and see who had the clearest visions, and whose dreams came true.

Alastair Fothergill
Executive Producer / Director
BBC / Great Ape Productions Ltd

The Blue Planet
Planet Earth
Frozen Planet

I am the Executive Producer of *Frozen Planet*, working with the Series Producer, Vanessa Berlowitz. I do that for half the year as a BBC staff member, and for the other half of the year I am working on two cinema release movies for Disney through my own company: one on African cats with Keith Scholey and one on chimpanzees with Mark Linfield.

If you look back at the history of wildlife film-making, I think it has always been changing and to a certain extent there have always been technological changes. Inevitably we are an industry shaped, to a certain extent, by technology. You could point, for example, to the Cineflex as being a big breakthrough on *Planet Earth* and time-lapse a big breakthrough on *The Private Life of Plants;* there will always be technical breakthroughs. They allow imaginative film-makers to conquer new barriers

What interests me more is the creative challenge of film-making and I do think that has changed over the last ten years owing to a number of factors. It's a much more competitive market that it used to be; there is an enormous variety of media that people can choose from, not just television, but online etc. The old days of knowing that twenty million people would sit down and watch *Life on Earth* have gone because of this multi-channel environment, and so you have to work much harder to do something that is of significance and that is noticed by lots of people. At the same time, unfortunately, the money (there is only so much money that's available in the market) is now spread much thinner. There are so many more channels and people squabbling for that money – and a lot of those people, a lot of those broadcasters, lack ambition, in my view. They go for the safe option – and there are a number of ways to make cheaper wildlife films. I'm not being disparaging about those; I believe that it's a bit like food: you don't always want a main meal, you want fast food occasionally and I happened to have made my career in the sort of landmark area that you could describe as the main meal. But I have worked in all sorts of other areas of television and I don't think any one is easier than the other: I think making a very good presenter-led show is a very demanding skill, and making very good children's programmes is a very great skill – and so is making great landmark television. But it has been increasingly hard to get the money and the ambition to do the big landmark pieces that break out, and that I have been lucky enough to be associated with.

One aspect that I think is very exciting is that at the moment we are driven, very strongly, by the need to deliver an audience on the first television transmission. When most of the money comes from BBC1, the BBC expect *Frozen Planet* to deliver six million viewers and Discovery (where they've found that their repeats are no longer so successful, you really have to deliver) even more. That has meant that some people have been forced into a very aggressive up-front, battle against the desire to change channel. We're in the channel-switching age!

However, you look at the DVD sales of *Planet Earth,* it's now the highest selling factual DVD ever: over five million DVDs in the States. What's exciting about that is they can watch it without the advertisements, and they can watch it time and time and time again. Unlike drama and comedy, one of the things about natural history is that people do want to own it, they do want to look at it many times, they do want their children to have it: so I think that the new technology could be fantastic for us.

If you can make a business plan where just download made it pay, and that could easily happen, then you are no longer controlled by the tyranny of the demands of the broadcaster. It will allow you to make a really beautiful natural world film that is never going to do more than a million on BBC1, and probably won't find a home in the States. But actually if lots of people buy that DVD because they like it, or download it because they like it, it is another way of financing things which is particularly suited to the sort of programming that we want to do. That doesn't apply to programmes like soap operas or *Strictly Come Dancing*

– those are about the event, whereas our shows' real interest and their real life is in the tale, and the technology making that happen.

DVDs were barely around ten years ago and yet most of the money that's invested in top-end natural history now is based on the money that's going to come back from DVD sales. I know the DVD market is going down but it's being replaced by download. It doesn't make any difference – it's the same money.

That's also very interesting for the young guy who goes out and says 'I want to make my little kingfisher film on a small camera and I want to edit it at home on my computer and I want to put it out on the internet, put it out on YouTube' – I think that's very exciting.

As far as the increasing resolution of cameras and formats goes, our eyes have a limit of resolution, there's no doubt about that. At its very top end we're almost there in the resolution of the collecting; the very top-end cameras are of extraordinarily high resolution now. The problem is that once you start broadcasting, the process of getting that resolution to the screen goes down. Most 'high-definition' televisions are not high-definition! There are so many problems to overcome along the line after acquisition, that the only way you can react is to say, 'Well let's acquire in the very highest quality format that we can because everything is going to be worse from then on'. It's driven principally by the makers of the cameras who very deliberately put out lower quality cameras in stages. They never release their top-end camera now because they want to sell all the nearly-top-end cameras first.

Planet Earth was the first HD series that had been made, and when I was told I had to do it in HD I was, frankly, terrified. But I'm absolutely delighted that we did it. And those cameramen, who at the beginning of *Planet Earth* said, "I hate this, it's a video camera, it's ugly": if you told them they had to go back to Super 16 and they couldn't see their rushes on location, they wouldn't like it! When I made *Life in the Freezer*, I went to Antarctica for twelve weeks and spent a third of my whole series budget without seeing a single frame until I got home. Nowadays that would never work. I am pushing my directors in the field, telling them I don't just want the shots, I want the story, I want a storyboard, I want them to come back with a sequence that's got narrative, that's got power and will work in the cutting room: and to do that, being able to see rushes in the field is very important.

35mm is still the highest resolution format on the market but it has a relatively short life left. I think in natural history Super 16 is dead. I

159

would never go back to film.

I think 3D is over-rated. Natural history is about taking people to the place. It's an immersive medium, if you get it right. There is no doubt that well done 3D can be very immersive; I think *Avatar* was a very well made 3D film. The trouble is, lots of films that have so far been produced in 3D were done so purely for box office reasons – and they are not very good 3D. But if you look at the box office, people are not willing to pay extra for 3D. If you are paying $5 extra and there's a whole family of four, that's an extra $20 – quite a lot of money! As a business, I don't think 3D is anywhere near as important as people thought it was after *Avatar*.

Then you have the problem, as the film-maker, when you are trying to record new behaviour, trying to film things that have never been seen before. There are good reasons why these things haven't been filmed before, and you are often on the edge of technology, you are pushing the boundaries. You have to have real mobility and at the moment, almost all the 3D rigs really limit your ability to get on top of the behaviour. You can always go and film a number of more predictable, easy things, but you're never going to get a snow leopard in 3D, you are never going to get some of the footage we got on *Frozen Planet* on 3D, so you have to take all that into account.

The other interesting thing is that as 3D rigs improve in quality, so does dimensionalisation (the process of making images or film that was not filmed in 3D visible with the illusion of the third dimension). You could well find that you spend five years developing the very best 3D rig only to realise that actually you could have shot it in 2D and dimensionalised it!

There are certain people in our industry who get very excited by new technology and say that wildlife film-making is all about new technology, but I think the dog should wag the tail and editorial should lead. The reason that the Cineflex was very successful on *Planet Earth* was not because it was an amazing piece of technology but because it delivered on the editorial; in that case it was a film about places, about how animals survive in these habitats.

For example, traditionally we'd film polar bears at ground level, but that way you don't understand the world that polar bears live in. If you can get up in the air, and you can pull back and back and see that this animal lives on an ice sheet, an endless ice sheet, where it has absolutely no camouflage from its prey – and any minute the world it's walking on is about to melt beneath its feet – suddenly, emotionally and editorially, you understand polar bears. That's why Cineflex worked for *Planet Earth.*

There is a danger in our industry that people get hyped about technology and actually it's the wrong way round. What you have to say is: I want to show people that plants move, therefore I'm going to develop amazing motion-control time-lapse. It's not the other way around. If technology allows us to tell stories I'll be the first one to try and use it but I think we talk too much about technology and we talk very little about storytelling.

Featuring humans in wildlife films will never go away; the first films had people in them and the trend goes up and down in phases. But it's sad that in some cases it's been a way to make cheap television and it's sad that it's been a way to exploit animals. There's a lot in that area that is hyped danger (??), which I wish we weren't doing. It's a cheap trick and I don't think it's true to the nature. I don't think animals are dangerous, I think the people who film them are far more dangerous.

However I think there is a real role for presenters in films if they allow the audience to experience the place or the animal better. Some of David Attenborough's very best sync pieces are about the animal. David never ever says "I", he never talks about his emotions, he talks about the animal and about the place. That allows people to travel emotionally with him and I think good presenters will always do that.

With regards to conservation films, I think they are an amazing challenge and I really admire the people who make them well. We all know the state of the planet, we all know it's a massive issue, and I have personally been criticised that series like *Planet Earth* show the world through rose-tinted spectacles. If *Planet Earth* were the only sort of film out there, then I would totally agree with that. But nobody had ever seen a snow leopard before and I still think that there is a market and a new generation every year that needs to see the natural world.

We're an increasingly urban population globally. More people live in cities than ever before and these people will never see the natural world. How can they care about it if we don't make beautiful films that transport them there? That said, I also think there is a real market for extremely good journalism, but I think a lot of us, because we care about these issues so much, have become a bit lazy in the communication. We just think that because this is an important thing to say, we don't have to bother to say it well. Unfortunately in this

161

increasingly competitive and demanding world of multimedia you absolutely have to say it well because there are so many people crying wolf with environmental matters that the audience is almost cynical about it. Getting them to understand the plight of the polar bear for example: It's a real challenge and I immensely admire people that make very powerful, effective conservation films. I think the need for them is desperate.

Sophie Vartan
Founder, CEO and Executive Producer, NHU Africa
Founder and Director Wildlife Film Academy
Founder and Managing Director Wild Talk Africa Film Festival

Into the Dragon's Lair (co-production Animal Planet)
Dragon's Feast 3D
Cheetah Diaries (in its 4th season)

As Chief Executive of the Natural History Unit of Africa (NHU Africa) my perspectives are influenced by ideas and developments in Southern Africa. Because I commission local productions, as well as co-produce with, and distribute to, international broadcasters, I am fortunate enough to be exposed to the international standards of natural history programming worldwide as well. This puts me in a position where it is important for our company to be communicating industry trends and requirements to the fast-growing African wildlife film-making industry. Our Wildlife Film Academy (www.wildlifefilmacademy.com) is a great crash-course for newcomers, and we try to update our content according to latest developments and trends. Hosting Africa's only international wildlife film festival biennially, Wild Talk Africa (www.wildtalkafrica.com) is also integral in connecting our local community with key international players, as well as showcasing local skills and stories. We are honoured to be able to host an event that fosters a sense of community and progressive action for African wildlife film-makers to keep up with the highly competitive international audience.

The industry has undergone so many changes and developments, in the last ten years, that it is difficult to isolate what has had the greatest impact. The explosion of digital film-making is the most obvious change. With the HD format becoming the industry standard, and the incredible developments in cameras now available to the 'pro-sumer' market, we have witnessed a huge increase in the number of newcomers to the wildlife film-making industry. Film was an expensive and exclusive format, but the digital age has freed up the market to anyone with the drive and commitment to make a career in this field. This has been wonderful for us at NHU Africa, as well as for our Film Academy students, and it has positively affected our budgeting process.

The incredible advances in technology have enabled us to make use of high-speed cameras for remarkable imagery, such as in our film *The Nature of Life*. We are also in production of our first 3D film, *Dragon's Feast*, and that has been an exciting journey. However it has been very important for us carefully to understand how 3D production and workflows affect budgets and schedules, and to minimise risks by using only a crew accustomed to the format. The idea of conventional 'typical wildlife cameras' is also disappearing – film-makers are creating films that pass broadcast quality requirements with low cost and innovative cameras, which retail at a tenth of the price of conventional wildlife cameras. Some film-makers are even producing films on DSLR stills cameras.

We have also witnessed the move away from observational wildlife films to those strongly rooted in characters, narrative and story. Technology has lent itself to more intimate exchanges with subjects, resulting in deeper stories on human-animal interaction. NHU Africa's commissioning brief is very oriented towards this. Still popular are the animal rescue programs, and those about people who have special affinities or unique relationships with the animal world. *Meerkat Manor* from Animal Planet started the trend in human narratives over a natural back-drop, touching the audience on a deeper level than traditional observational wildlife programs. When NHU Africa produced our award-winning *A Kalahari Tail* – which profiled ground squirrels of the Kalahari – adding a human sub-narrative allowed for the audience to be captivated by the behaviour of the ground squirrels.

Another exciting development for natural history programming is the growth of an expedition and adventure slant to the genre. *Into the*

Dragon's Lair has won two prestigious international awards in the category of 'Expedition/Adventure', a category we have also added to our Wild Talk Africa Roscar film awards (www.wildtalkafrica.com). Pushing and exploring the boundaries within natural history programming is important for the growth of the industry, and means the genre can be distributed to alternative broadcasters and reach new audiences.

Distribution trends have changed the nature of our programming with the incredible advance in online distribution. Social media have made news immediate, communication between different territories and culture infinite. The infamous *Battle of the Kruger* – filmed with a small handycam – goes to show the power in the reach of the internet with respect to wildlife film-making. This has infinite implications for the rogue wildlife film-maker. The internet has also made crowd-funding possible. People can find funding for their films through websites such as IndieGoGo.com and Kickstarter.com. Wildlife production companies have started daily wildlife podcasts, video-blogs and YouTube channels. TV and cinema is now not the dominant and autonomous platform for people to seek wildlife imagery. Even Facebook has exploded with wildlife groups, exhibiting both still and moving images. Distribution can now be immediate and the power is in the hands of the individual. In the face of broadcasters' budgets' being cut, and various industries being affected by the global economy pressures, new distribution channels mean more content and not less. If anything, the next ten years will see more wildlife content produced than ever before.

So where does our industry head over the next ten years? We cannot deny that in terms of wildlife and the natural world, wilderness, habitats and species are under threat. Additionally, new stories for captivating programming are becoming harder to come by. But at NHU Africa we see this as an opportunity to get creative and discover new angles. We also still believe that, certainly in Africa, there are many untold stories that still need to see the light of day. The shifts in TV are difficult to predict, but this also allows for freedom and ingenuity for film-makers. There is space to define new trends, become brave and take risks regarding narratives and content themes.

Some quick advice for newcomers to the industry:

• If you are brand new to wildlife film-making you may need to consider being willing to volunteer in the industry for a short time. Hard work, dedication and creativity will take you far.

• Sign up with industry publications and read them more than you read the newspaper! A few helpful sites to follow (some are, of course, specific to the African film industry): Screen Africa, The Callsheet, Filmmakers' Guide to South Africa, AV Specialist, Africa Geographic, WorldScreen, Realscreen and FilmContact.com – to name a few.

• Attend film festivals – they are absolutely essential for networking and meeting key people in the industry, and allow opportunities to update yourself on the state of the industry. They also provide opportunities to pitch ideas and acquire priceless information through workshops and seminars. Festivals to watch are Wildscreen, Jackson Hole, International Wildlife Film Festival (Missoula), Japan Wildlife Film Festival and, of course, Wild Talk Africa here in South Africa.

• Get internet savvy – make sure you have an online presence for yourself or your company! Explore what is possible online, as an alternative funding or distribution source when you cannot get commissioned and distributed through the traditional channels.

• Be bold with your ideas – the conventions of our genre are being broken all the time. Broadcasters and commissioners are looking for truly unique narratives.

• And of course ... sign up for the Wildlife Film Academy to get a head start in this competitive industry (www.wildlifefilmacademy.com)!

Good luck!

Emma Rigney
Director of Development, Natural History
National Geographic Television

My role as Director of Development for Natural History at National Geographic Television is to find and develop factual program ideas (involving animals) for the National Geographic Channels, including its new wildlife channel, WILD.

My career in wildlife films began as a producer for the BBC Natural History Unit in the UK, so I've been in the business for over ten years now and in that time I've seen some shifts in the genre of natural history.

Technology is by far the biggest influence I've seen shaping wildlife film-making. HD cameras, new camera rigs, better lenses, night filming and small 'critter cams' have allowed us to reveal an animal's secret world. They pretty much have no privacy now!

The future of wildlife shows will depend on budgets, of course, but there will be a demand for new and interesting stories as well as new ways of seeing things, including in 3D. Flexibility in ways of filming things will be crucial and the willingness to go it alone without any reliable financial backing may be sometimes necessary. Passion, determination, story-telling skills and a good eye are vital for making excellent films.

Designing an original and entertaining approach to a subject we've already seen many times is always a challenge. Conservation stories can still be told, but just don't use the word 'conservation'. People want to be informed and told a good yarn: if you hook them with that then you may have a new person who cares about the underlying message.

The audience out there will always want to be reminded of how spectacular our planet is, but they also demand a fresh approach and always want to learn something new.

Neil Harraway
EVP Marketing and Development
NHNZ

The View from the Bottom of the World

I don't see much future for natural history film-making. I do see more future for making wildlife TV shows. I see quite a difference between them ...

I also see the future in 3D – though when, and how fully 3D it will be, I don't know. I see lower budgets, and higher budgets. I see both bright innovation and stubborn adherence to blue-chip tradition.

You need to know that I see the future and the world through NHNZ's lens of free-market competition as an autonomous production company.

THAT WAS THEN

NHNZ started in 1978, sheltered within a state-owned broadcaster, albeit one with modest budgets. We could learn our craft and build a track record and then launch into the world at the same time as Discovery did.

In our first twenty years life we saw little change – the voice of God (and Sir David's) rang out strongly and the chips were all blue, and that suited all broadcasters. In the last fifteen years there has been a lot of change – many other voices have been tried out, green-chip or red-chip (infused with adrenaline and blood) have been aired, and we have adapted to 'blue-cheap'.

In the past ten years NHNZ has felt all the same changes as freelancers in America – because that has been our main market. Discovery fell off all but the most 'muscular' natural history, and Animal Planet took the nature shows but then become more and more populist and less animal-driven (as per their slogan *Surprisingly Human*). Nat Geo Wild

167

start up globally then launched in the US in early 2010, and took all but the biggest animal programming from the core National Geographic Channel. Smithsonian channel started out modestly and started growing. PBS has suffered through financial woes but continues with their small and strong *Nature* series.

We have felt changes in Europe's terrestrial broadcasters. ZDF in Germany pulled their daily wildlife show. Slots on ZDF and the ARD channels went more to German producers and less to international co-pros. In France, Canal Plus and France3 moved away from international wildlife shows, leaving France5 as the strongest user, if modest payer. Arte continued to seek some wildlife co-production. In Britain, Channel 5's ownership changed and wobbled on their populist wildlife output. Even the BBC NHU was trimmed and trimmed but still continues to put out its usual blockbusters. And the world's other huge broadcast player, NHK of Japan, cut its weekly wildlife show from one hour to half an hour, but continues with its big specials.

THIS IS NOW

Because America is our primary market (NZ having too many sheep and not enough people to be a strong TV market) we follow, or try to anticipate, programming trends, like most prodcos. We all clambered on archive shows some years back, which satiated the public's appetite for natural history. We all pitched Alaska shows and now we're all pitching swamp shows ... *Swamp Wars* and *Swamp Men* and *Swamp People* and so on and on. In other genres we've seen Thom Beers rule the world of blue-chip ob-docs (observational documentaries) and have all tried to knock him off his throne. We've seen *Pawn Stars* and other treasure-hunting fact-ent (factual entertainment) series take a recession-hit America by storm, and all tried to find similar series.

Where natural history film-making once ruled the world, these hits in other genres show how cable TV networks are going more and more for entertainment-first series, as cable has grown to be fully accepted by the American viewing public. Series, and especially hosted or character-full series, grow loyal viewers and ratings more than one-off docos do, plus they are more cost-efficient. This applies to wildlife programming too and has driven the change to fact-ent animal shows.

Watching and feeling the changing world, NHNZ has covered its wild bets, like most prodcos, by diversifying into other genres such as science, history, adventure etc. But within wildlife, we also do animal archive shows, hosted populist shows and whatever new wrinkle we can find to stay in the game. We have, however, stuck with one-hour wildlife docos and series as we have been able to fund them – two notable achievements recently have been *Shark Nicole* for National Geographic and the *Life Force* aka *Mutant Planet* series with NHK/France Televisions/Science Channel/Animal Planet.

WHAT'S NEXT

In the next ten years I don't know what will happen to wildlife TV shows, but I reckon that if both the pace of change and the pace of TV shows keep accelerating we'll chase ourselves in smaller and faster circles on story and style until our heads swallow our tails and our tails swallow our heads ...

Technically – full tapeless production is inevitable: NHNZ has got into tapeless shooting and is gearing up for full tapeless post-production.
3D will become easier – ie more affordable, less cumbersome, 'one-piece' cameras. What I don't know is how deeply 3D will penetrate into the TV world ... partly it will be dictated by when glasses-free 3D sets are good enough and cheap enough for viewers. NHNZ has leapt into twenty hours of 3D series and we have learned there is some way to go before it is a full alternative to the 2D HD way.

Convergence of internet and TV is inevitable, which challenges us all: broadcasters because audience share will keep slipping, and subscriptions and advertising revenue will keep slipping; and producers because deals will become more fragmented in order to stitch together a viable budget. There might be a few stand-out hold-outs such as BBC and NHK and Discovery and A&E who can take all rights and exploit all possible media, but even they are not immune to the free-market pressures of the future. Blockbuster shows or series will continue to stand out, and just a few broadcasters and producers will be able to pull together the partnerships needed for blockbuster budgets.

User-generated content vs professional productions? Amateurs will gather some remarkable footage because they are in the right place at the right time. I think aspiring pros will find it easier to get a toehold in the digital world but harder to climb the slippery slope of professional success because there will be more competition and lower budgets. I think established professionals will continue to do well (within the limits of broadcasters' appetites and ability to pay) because of their assured quality and, more importantly, their storytelling ability.

SO WHAT?

What advice can I give young film-makers? Do whatever you can to get into the business – from the ground up, or from a tertiary course. NHNZ supports a science communication course here at Otago University. We commit to two interns per year from that, and we have employed many more as researchers or APs or camera ops – and a few have gone on to be producer/directors. But there are a lot of tertiary courses in communications, film, science etc pumping out an awful lot of students for not a lot of nat hist film jobs. In a Darwinian sense this is OK because the hungriest and the fittest do succeed.

If you really want to be a 'natural history film-maker' you obviously will target the broadcasters of classic wildlife films: BBC, NHK, PBS Nature, ARD, France Televisions, Arte, ORF ... or you could go for even purer authored films for the festival circuit and self-fund them through family fortune, foundations, angel investors – or the time-honoured begging, borrowing, scrimping and making do ...

If, however, you are fine with making wildlife TV shows for the masses, then be ready to seek out great hosts and characters, try bright new approaches of animal fact-ent, pitch hard, run fast and be ready to change direction as quickly as broadcasters may want.

But of course I may be wrong. There may be a huge resurgence of global popularity in blue-chip nature documentaries. We old-skool types could then shuffle off happily into the HD tapeless 3D sunset and the young enthusiasts could enjoy one of the best professions ever – until the next change. I venture that such a huge resurgence of interest would be led by a huge personality – another Cousteau or Attenborough or Irwin. Or by a game-changing rule-breaking butt-kicking revolution of a yet unknown kind – the Google or Facebook of wildlife TV – which one bright spark imagines. I hope that's you ...

Shinichi Murata
Executive Producer
NHK (Japan Broadcasting Corporation)

Satoyama
Equator
Life Force

Diversity: the key to a bright future for natural history television

I've been making natural-history programs for the Japanese public broadcaster NHK for nearly thirty years. I'm currently an executive producer for nature documentaries, some of which are international co-productions. My recent work includes *Life Force*, a series of six one-hour episodes that NHK produced in 2010 in partnership with Science Channel, Animal Planet, France Télévisions, and NHNZ. The *Life Force* series focuses on six of the thirty-four biodiversity hotspots that are home to especially significant populations of endangered species, and it presents some of the planet's most amazing creatures.

The most dramatic changes that I've seen in natural history television have come in the past ten years. They've been driven by two phenomena: a shift toward bigger productions; and rapid advances in digital technology. I see the BBC's 2005 series *Planet Earth* as a turning point. Collaboration with the film industry and big American cable channels gave *Planet Earth* a level of funding that had previously been inconceivable. Lots of production companies and television stations have followed the BBC's example by incorporating multi-platform delivery into their plans for major series. Digital technologies such as 4K and 3D have accelerated the trend, bringing down the barriers between the television and film industries in the natural-history field. The speed of advances in digital technologies can be perplexing. For instance, it's confusing to have so many 3D formats. But, at the same

171

time, it's exciting to see technology creating so many possibilities for new programming.

The changes I've mentioned are also a cause for concern. The cost of making a major series has made international co-production essential. The huge funding and market potential in the United States have become indispensable, so I'm concerned that the storytelling approaches and program-making cultures that are unique to particular countries could be diluted and homogenized. There's a risk that all productions will eventually look the same, so I think it's more important than ever for documentary-makers to strive to tell strong stories from new and diverse perspectives.

NHK has always endeavoured to break new ground. For instance, I began working fifteen years ago on the *Satoyama* documentary series, which highlights environmentally sustainable lifestyles. There are three *Satoyama* episodes, the second of which won a Prix Italia and the International Wildlife Film Festival's best-of-festival award in 2005. The series has none of the drama of documentaries about lions or dinosaurs; it's a gentle presentation of rural Japanese people, living in harmony with nature rather than trying to control it. Our storytelling may be a little slow for westerners, but our message about sustainable lifestyles has clearly struck a chord with people around the world. In fact, the awareness created by the *Satoyama* series was largely to thank for the adoption of the Satoyama Initiative at the United Nations biodiversity summit in Nagoya in 2010.

The *Life Force* series also highlights the importance of diversity in program styles. It's aimed mainly at terrestrial television in France and Japan, but has also been a hit on US cable television. One reason for its popularity is that it's a cross-genre fusion of blue-chip natural-history storytelling and scientific investigation. There's brilliant photography of aspects of nature that had never been seen on television; experts on evolutionary science describe their latest findings; and scientific theories and phenomena are clearly demonstrated by computer-generated images. NHK's co-production partners were initially worried that frequent use of scientists and CGIs in a blue-chip natural-history series wouldn't appeal to western audiences, but this approach was quite common in Japan. We at NHK saw it as a great way to break away from conventional natural history programming, which tends to be relatively strong on photography but relatively weak on storytelling. The approach we took with *Life Force* also gives viewers of all ages a unique chance to engage with the issues of evolution and biodiversity, and it appeals to lots of people who had never been interested in natural history. Our co-production partners are as delighted as our viewers. At the end of the day, the keys to a bright future for natural-history television are fresh production approaches and strong, unique stories. Just as genetic diversity helps species to adapt and survive, diversity in program-making will ensure that our industry survives and thrives.

Xi Zhinong
Founder
Wild China Film

Mysteries of Yunnan Snub-nosed Monkey (winner of TVE Award of 2002 Wildscreen Film Festival)

Wild China Film has recently launched China's Endangered Species Photography Project (CESPP), a non-profit project aimed at sponsoring Chinese photographers to film China's fast-disappearing, yet little-known, endemic species, and using the photos to promote conservation of those species. So far CESPP has sponsored over twenty projects and the chosen species include Tibetan fox, newly-discovered amphibian species, endemic Chinese pheasants, etc.

Having thirty years of wildlife filming experience in China, I am currently leading a team of experienced wildlife photographers to film the most difficult and the most endangered species in China, such as Tibetan antelope, snub-nosed monkeys, big cats, gibbons, parrots, etc.

First of all, wildlife film-making has not become an industry in China yet. In the last ten years, since Wild China Film was founded, we have endeavoured to promote the development of this industry in China by giving over fifty lectures every year, accepting numerous media interviews, organising wildlife photography training camps and exhibitions, etc. Now China has a large number of amateur nature photographers and a growing number of professional wildlife photographers. The amazing evolution of digital equipment in the last decade, as well as the internet, has made this progress possible.

I think wildlife film-making will become an industry in China in the next ten years. And our CESPP will capture images of most of the red-listed species in China by then. Through wide spreading of images those species will receive more public attention, and we must hope their status will be improved by better conservation efforts.

Although the wildlife film-making industry has become a mature industry in western countries, and lots of species and places have been filmed, there still exist many species and places that are unknown to the world outside China. As wildlife film-makers we should maintain our curiosity and spirit of exploration, and try our best to bring the latest information about nature to the world.

Jackson Xu
Images Biodiversity Expedition Ins. (IBE)
China

Is Chinese Wildlife Film-making likely to catch-up with the rest of the world?

Wild China (BBC NHU 2008)
Biodiversity of Shiqu Highland (FFI&IBE 2010)
Yarlung Tsangpo Grand Canyon Quest (IBE 2010)

I think, in ten years' time, there may be a chance for China to catch up with the rest of the world in the wildlife film-making industry, as technology and markets develop. But some conditions are necessary: sustainable business models, professional production teams, and excellent leaders. If any of them are missing, China will act only as an audience in this genre.

In China people started to watch wildlife films through *Animal World* on CCTV (China Central Television) from the end of 1981 (this TV series ceased about ten years ago). *Animal World* consisted mostly of programmes from the BBC NHU, and gave a lot of inspiration to

175

Chinese people, including me.

In 1998 an International Nature Film Week was launched in Beijing, and I had the chance to see lot of excellent natural history documentaries, including Hugh Miles's *Puma: Lion of the Andes*. These films impressed me deeply, and led me to determine to join the wildlife film-making industry in China. I then worked as a natural history editor for *Chinese National Geography* magazine from 2000 to 2006, worked as Chief Researcher for the BBC NHU *Wild China* series in 2006, and, at the same time, helped to establish *Wild China Film* studio with Mr Xi Zhinong.

In 2008 I took the lead to establish Images Biodiversity Expedition Ins., to produce picture albums and natural history films for Chinese nature reserves and National Parks (government and NGOs). In 2009 I translated Piers Warren's book *Go Wild with Your Camcorder: How to make Wildlife Films,* which became the first book about wildlife film-making in China.

In the last ten years Chinese audiences have seen a lot of wildlife films on TV (most produced by BBC, National Geographic, Discovery, ABC, NHNZ and NHK). The main reason for this was that the TV station managed to get the broadcast rights for relatively low prices. I estimate the broadcast programmes amounted to about 300 hours per year. Another reason was that China had produced only a few good native documentaries about our own wildlife. The native wildlife programmes from all TV stations in China totalled about 100 hours per year. The format was normally hosting in studio plus a story from the field; the content mostly novelty-seeking with a lack of visual impact, scientific accuracy or care for nature. As a result Chinese audiences know more about the African elephant than about the giant panda.

There were some relatively good native programmes, but the output was very small, about five hours per five years, and with high cost. Most of them received special governmental funding, but without a successful business model became unsustainable and unstable. With the lack of successful sustainable business models, Chinese wildlife film-making still does not have stable professional production teams. Some teams have strong human-based documentary and news programme experience, but have not enough biological background.

In the past ten years this industry has changed from 16mm film production to HD technology. Shooting costs will continue to decrease and broadcast technology and approach will become more diverse. But despite the changes I think high quality and powerful wildlife films still need higher finance, long production times, and experienced teams. So, in the coming ten years, most high-quality films will still come from big experienced companies. They could take the lead to establish new successful business models to match the developing technology. But, at the same time, small-scale companies and low-budget projects should be able reach more audiences with their strong individuality.

My hope and advice to this industry in China: in the next ten years we have the chance to catch up with the world in the wildlife film-making genre as technology and market conditions vary significantly. But this will need several key conditions: innovative sustainable business models, professional and stable production teams, and energetic and experienced leaders.

Dennis Aig
Professor and Program Head
MFA in Science and Natural History Filmmaking

Deep Gulf Wrecks (podcasts, PAST Foundation)
Visions of Grace: Robert Redford and 'The Horse Whisperer' (Buena Vista Television/Lifetime)
Test Pilots of the Body (Hunter Neil Company/Montana Public Television)

No Guru, No Method, No Teacher
(with apologies to Van Morrison)

The digital upheaval that has swept through media production over the past two decades has rocked wildlife film-making out of its comfortable 'niche' status. No longer simply an exercise in education or adventure, wildlife films find themselves forced by both aesthetics and economics to embrace genres they often carefully avoided: reality television, social documentary, advocacy media, and even fiction film-making. While probably always marketable in one form or another, the traditional program, with a voice-of-God narrator explaining beautiful shots, seems like the last gasp of a doomed *ancien régime*. The new technology also allows individuals to originate and distribute programs without relying on the traditional organizational pillars of wildlife production. While these developments will eventually wipe away many of the familiar characteristics of the wildlife film, they also promise to expand, modernize, and revitalize a kind of production that has often lapsed into lockstep predictability.

I am currently a Professor of Film and Photography at Montana State University and the Program Head of our MFA in Science and Natural History Filmmaking, a unique program founded ten years ago by my predecessor, Professor Ronald Tobias. I also continue to work actively in production, usually in the role of producer, production manager, or director. I also serve as Executive Producer of *TERRA: The Nature of Our World*, a graduate-student managed podcast and website that has enjoyed ten million downloads in its five years of existence.

178

In both my academic and production positions, I spend a considerable amount of time anticipating the future of science and natural history film-making. I have concluded that both teachers and students must approach major changes with open-mindedness and enthusiasm. I once advised my students in a very impromptu comment during a lecture to "embrace the chaos" that inevitably infuses a production. I believe that is still the best way to surf the waves of change, so you can understand them while also learning how to adapt to them. Resistance will be met with a swift wipeout.

As with most transformative events, the digital era requires the redefinition of who we are and what we do. Are we still 'film-makers' if we no longer use film, but instead create digital files stored on drives or memory cards, and rely on software to do everything from fixing our exposure errors to editing? Until we reach a consensus on a new term (probably through social networks and tweets) our current terminology will have to do, but its life expectancy is undoubtedly short.

We also need to talk about productions differently. We tell each other that old and new media share the need for 'storytelling'. This narrative basis is undoubtedly true, but the focus, by implicitly invoking authors from Rowling to the Mother Goose story, ignores the way new technology inevitably modifies human perception, especially in the critical areas of time, space, and movement.

The digital era has also initiated great democratization. With the widespread use of computers, inexpensive cameras, and mobile phones in even remote communities, there is a profound shift in the creator-audience relationship. A production is no longer an end unto itself: it is the beginning of a conversation that can often involve millions of people. In the multiplatform world, the audience insists on becoming an active part of a production through blogs, postings, tweets, social networks, and other means. The formerly-anonymous audience now has a voice that will express opinions with far more impact than the ratings and other older methods that relied on quantitative gauges of audience reactions.

This large, international audience also expects much more of producers. A program or series is no longer sufficient on its own: it becomes the center of an information galaxy of photos, histories, timelines, behind-the-scenes footage, blogs, hyperlinks, social network outlets, games, and other digital media. All these elements create what has become known as the 360-degree web world of the production.

The changes in media production and presentation are already creating

179

a profound evolution in how we look at wild places and creatures. With 24/7 access to information about once-unseen wildlife and remote environments, viewers as well as film-makers will no longer accept the idea of any wild place not having had at least some human impact on it. Humans, it seems, have insinuated themselves everywhere on the planet and beyond. Natural history, as a result, is morphing into the study of how people and nature interact. It is no longer simply the documentation of wild creatures in Edenic isolation.

Perhaps the greatest change will be that in the future both film-makers and their audiences will be 'digital natives'. They will access programming through the web, not through traditional broadcasters or cable and satellite organizations. They will also be creating media images from a very young age. A fourteen-year-old in many countries today has the same knowledge of film-making that most members of my generation did not acquire until college or graduate school. This group also communicates through short films posted to Facebook, YouTube, or HD cell phone video. Moving-image-making is their *lingua franca*. The young people are youthful one-person production and distribution organizations. The individuals who live in the Himalayas, on the Serengeti, or within the Arctic Circle are making films about the wildlife they interact with daily. The images may not be breathtakingly blue-chip, but the perspectives and insights in these videos may very well be world-changing.

In any time of upheaval, disruption of the prevailing norms may be seen as either a threat or as liberation from restrictions. As the recent Arab Spring movements demonstrated, the revolution will not only be televised, it will be tweeted, blogged, uplinked, open-meshed and crowd-sourced. The media revolution easily transcends borders and cultures, to be truly international. Most excitingly for natural history film-makers, moving imagery is at the center of it, with wildlife and habitats a major issue of worldwide importance.

In this onslaught of change, future film-makers (or whatever they will ultimately be called) need flexibility, open-mindedness, and a daily dedication to solving the multitude of problems that will arise. They will need to know the past as one step in figuring out the future. While at present there is no guru, no method, and no teacher offering a path of certainty and security, there will be a guiding logic emerging from the millions of individual digital experiments and productions. The future will definitely not be as simple as romancing someone in Van Morrison's spiritual garden wet with rain, but it does hold out the same promise of achieving new levels of intellectual, artistic, and spiritual fulfillment.

180

Chris Palmer
Professor / Wildlife Film Producer
Director of the Center for Wildlife Filmmaking

As an 11-year old in 1958 I watched the Disney film *White Wilderness*. In the film we see a cute little bear cub lose its footing on a steep, snow-covered mountainside and fall faster and faster until it's tumbling down totally out of control. It eventually stops falling after banging hard into rocks. The audience laughs because we assume it is totally natural and authentic and it's funny in a slapstick kind of way – at least at first. In fact, it is totally staged, top to bottom, including the use of a man-made artificial mountain and a captive bear cub.

What ethical issues does this story illustrate? First, audience deception through staging and manipulation. Second, cruelty to animals. And third, a more subtle ethical issue but a vital one nonetheless: do wildlife films encourage conservation?

I have learned over the years that audiences want wildlife films to be authentic, and they don't want film-makers to harm animals or their environments. As I explain in my book, *Shooting in the Wild: An Insider's Account of Making Movies in the Animal Kingdom*, when viewers discover that film-makers cause unnecessary suffering to an animal, or that the film is inauthentic or contrived, they feel cheated and misled. But the line is often blurry.

As film-makers we have to ask ourselves three questions: first, are audiences deceived and misled, and if so, does it matter? When does legitimate film-making artifice become unacceptable deception? I'm thinking here of fake sounds, the use of CGI manipulation, and captive animals that appear free-roaming. Recently I saw amazing footage of a cougar hunting down a bear cub. It looked genuine, not fake in any way, but in fact it had all been carefully scripted and shot with trained animals from game farms. Other deceptions include the temptations to exaggerate, overdramatize, and sentimentalize.

181

Second, are wild animals harassed and disturbed during filming? As the story about the bear cub in *White Wilderness* illustrates, animal harassment and cruelty have been pervasive in wildlife filming for decades. This harassment can take the form of everything from simply getting too close to wild animals and disturbing them, through to deliberate violence. In the old days, if a film-maker wanted to capture a hunting scene of a bobcat chasing a rabbit, it was standard practice to get the shot by the use of invisible filament around the rabbit's neck or leg to slow it down artificially. Luckily such overt abuse is now uncommon. However, many on-camera hosts like Jeff Corwin, Bear Grylls, or the late Steve Irwin still grab and harass animals in order to create entertainment.

And third, is conservation advanced by these films? It would be facile and misleading to claim that *The Cove* failed because it hasn't yet stopped the killing of dolphins in Taiji, Japan; or that *Food Inc.* failed because it has not yet led viewers to change their eating habits; or that *The End of the Line* failed because it has not yet reduced over-fishing in our oceans – facile and misleading because where you stand on that issue depends on where you sit. If you're a dolphin in Taiji about to be butchered, then you might well think the film has failed to advance conservation. But if you're a viewer moved by the film to demonstrate outside the barbed wire surrounding the cove where the slaughter takes place, and the press is covering you and more attention is being brought to the issue, then the film may seem like a success in terms of conservation.

Audience deception, animal harassment, and lack of conservation raise tough questions. But crossing the ethics line into the dark side is seductively tempting if you are working hard to build your career and support your family. However, film-makers of the future have the opportunity to make important, far-reaching, and highly rated films that avoid many, if not all, of the ethical quagmires mentioned above. Emerging film-makers have the ability to create engaging and memorable films built around captivating stories and characters without resorting to misleading audiences, harming animals, or omitting conservation. These films can faithfully show animals in their natural state and tell riveting stories that strengthen people's ties to the natural world. As I outlined in my book, there are several steps that need to be taken to reach this end.

First and foremost, we should improve the ethics training for student film-makers so, for example, placing the welfare of our subjects above all else becomes the default mode of film-making, and disclosing how our films are made in the credits becomes standard practice. Our old approaches have led us into ethically dubious behaviors, including getting the money shot at all costs, hiding from the audience some of the deceptions we use to get those money shots, and sometimes harassing animals to get the shots we need to attract a high rating. It is no longer acceptable to use animals from game farms clandestinely, employ CGI to manipulate images surreptitiously, or goad animals to jack up the on-screen dramatic tension. We must clean shop before a third party finds out what passes for the art and artifice of wildlife film-making and publishes their findings on the front page of a national newspaper.

Second, we need to use new media more effectively. The internet has provided an outlet for outsiders to voice their concerns on wildlife issues, but it can also be used by professional film-makers to circumvent networks like Discovery and National Geographic who are most guilty of producing irresponsibly sensational programming. Video sites like YouTube allow amateur and professional film-makers to post and view digital video clips in mere seconds, without difficulty. Moreover, advocacy groups can now use a video camera and website as a powerful weapon in their cause. Whether used for advocacy, entertainment, or education, the web-based film revolution will continue to open up new opportunities as millions more people carry phones and other devices that can capture video and generate content. The big challenge with the internet is how to make money as a film-maker.

Third, the wildlife film-making community must re-think its approach to making wildlife films. Creating conservation films that are captivating to audiences, even when the subject is grim, and telling compelling stories, would make broadcasters more willing to air them. Finding characters that face emotionally wrenching challenges can add drama to a film. Placed in extraordinary circumstances seemingly ordinary people, such as scientists, park rangers, and whistle blowers, can often increase ratings. Inspirational people on the screen can make conservation films more entertaining, helping people to feel motivated to get something done. Adding humor can grab viewers' attention and hold it long enough to deliver an important message. With a little fine-tuning, these approaches can obtain higher ratings, enlist more conservationists, and give viewers a strong connection to the natural world.

Film has such unique potential for impacting public opinion that it is irresponsible to produce over sensationalized and destructive programming. The ethical questions related to wildlife film-making are

183

not simple, but we must at least openly confront the issue of ethics instead of constantly pushing for ratings, no matter the cost. Wildlife film-makers have a responsibility to depict the natural world accurately and in a way that will inspire people to conserve it.

Janet Rose
Executive Director/Festival Director
International Wildlife Film Festival and Media Center

Hope in a Changing World:
The Role and Impact of Wildlife Film on Global Conservation,
Today, Tomorrow and the Next Ten Years

The title of this article was the theme of this past May's 34th International Wildlife Film Festival and it is fitting, I think, as we try to understand wildlife film-making today in the context of species- and habitat-loss, and as we look to the future. There have been, and continue to be, many debates about the idea of conservation as a key component of wildlife films and film-making: as a former television producer, head of conservation communications at an international conservation organization, and now wildlife film festival director, I have to come down on the side of saying *yes*, conservation is a critical component of wildlife films – and even more so as we go forward into an uncertain future.

While it is true that blue-chip natural history films without conservation – just pure, stunning cinematography, epic music, brilliant narration, and so on – might serve to inform and inspire, it is Conservation with a capital C that gives rise to hope, inspiration, storyline and a *reason* to care. To quote my dear and very good friend, Dr George Schaller, with whom I share this view, "people will only save what they care about," and caring, I think, comes from wildlife films that give us reason to hope, reason to be passionate about saving a species or a place, and help to inspire us to action. Overall, I think, this is the critical role of conservation in wildlife films.

Add to this idea the fact that the traditional model of wildlife conservation is changing – dramatically. Where conservation was once driven solely by science, today scientists must add other ingredients to the mix: people, their cultural traditions, the socio-political-economic ramifications of wildlife conservation – and a host of other related and intertwined influences. This is the new conservation model or approach, and if wildlife films are to reflect what is happening in the wildlife field then again all of these elements must be taken into consideration in the making of a film. This need not be exclusive or part of every wildlife film, but it should at least have a strong influence.

Until fairly recently asking a broadcaster to put conservation into a commercial wildlife film was anathema; many will still refuse. But increasingly broadcasters have come around, and now see the really good *stories* in conservation as part of a wildlife film. As a result, whether it is subtle or more direct, we see conservation becoming a part of wildlife films with greater frequency.

The flip side of this, according to one great field scientist with whom I shared this debate (Dr Iain Douglas-Hamilton), is that when you incorporate conservation into a wildlife film, you are making a claim for the human imperative. A film then is not just about the wildlife, but the people too. And Dr Douglas-Hamilton suggests, rightfully, that not every film has to include people. That is true, but it is where I think our human future and the future of wildlife, habitat and film-making converge. There is hardly a place on earth where wildlife is completely free from human interaction, human encounters, and human influence. So I don't think it is a bad thing to incorporate people into a wildlife

185

film and thus include conservation. I think it is almost vital.

As to the question of 'The Future', and what it means for the industry, this is where I see the future of wildlife film-making: a combination of wildlife, people, culture, human traditions and their impact on species. One example of this, which I think was done brilliantly, was the BBC film *Snow Leopard, Beyond the Myth*. This type of film I think is the bow-wave of the future and a wonderful example of where wildlife film-making is headed. But it is just one example of what I think of as *the new genre*. Other examples include Nature's *Wolverine*; Animal Planet's *Whale Wars*; National Geographic's *American Serengeti*, to name only a few: all contain varying degrees of *conservation*, the role of people and of course very different approaches and storylines.

Perhaps the most important thing to remember is that we -- as film-makers, conservationists and communicators -- are *thinking about* conservation in new ways and in the ways in which we communicate about it, its subjects and its importance We are thinking more and more about our roles in educating the public and raising awareness through television, film and the Internet. We are more willing than ever to explore new avenues, to think outside the box and to reach people. No one can say with certainty what exactly the future looks like, nor understand all the variables, but one thing is certain: the commitment, the wave of passionate film-making, is greater than ever. The future is, indeed, full of hope.

Mark Wild
Executive Producer
artists in motion

Wildlife film-making is at a crucial point now. It is more important than ever to draw an audience to the natural world and, in so doing, help appreciate and preserve its beauty and environment.

In some ways that becomes ever harder as an intelligent audience is increasingly looking for new angles and devices: broadcasters have to feed that need with commercial justification as well as rating success. Not only does it have to be good, but also it has to rate well, from the initial beautiful postcards from the world to adrenalin-driven fear and adventure with characters or voice-over. I would argue that, while the added chemistry draws new audiences, it might also instil a primal fear

– a short-term gain but a long-term loss, maybe. It's hard to say, and this fear may not be beneficial in the long run. However, you do need to provide a layer cake of emotions for the modern audience.

My entry into the industry was by default, as I was trained in film and had entered television for a day-job to earn money to fund more scripts and productions. I applied the principles of feature film and story in my job, which worked well in harvesting a new audience in commercial television: *Meerkat Manor* (a kind of '*Desperate Housewives* meets *Natural World*'), *Nick Baker's Weird Creatures*, *RSPCA – Have You Got What It Takes*, *Tiger Zero* (current affairs) or *Crime Scene Wild* (conservation in action). I think *Crime Scene Wild*, in 2006, melded real-time investigation with drama, education and results: as Steve Galster and agents carried covert cameras and we, the viewers, saw Mr Big with one thousand white shark dorsal fins in his warehouse, or tiger wine, for example.

I remember worrying for my job when a *Big Cats* episode got subpoenaed in the US, and then realised on reflection it was okay to have a documentary called for evidence; it meant you were doing your job and breaking new ground.

Amba the Russian Tiger was a 'film' really. The main protagonist, Gordon Buchanan, goes on a journey to find the elusive Siberia tiger, but never finds it; this was really the best conservation message, but it was not deemed the ideal pay off at the time as we, the audience, needed to see the tiger. Instead we saw Gordon find himself among the ancient forest people.

Gorilla School was pioneering, showing Damian Aspinall bringing baby gorillas back to their natural world after being born in captivity, and teaching them to be wild and free again.

I think, however, that the next generation of wildlife film-makers has the hardest task, for they need to continue to instil a curiosity and appreciation of our beautiful planet, but without preaching. More educating-by-default is needed, with something as well as entertainment; with enthrallment as the engagement tool. Maybe a simple narrative or charismatic character will no longer do, and instead we shall be vicariously entering the world around us, with the ever-present question, what is the story?

It will be a complex chemical cocktail of emotions – the alchemy of audience. Or is it easier just to keep it simple, and appeal to basic emotion? We are currently making a series for Channel 5 and BBC Worldwide called *Tarsier Towers* about the elusive primate Tarsiers that lives in the jungles of Indonesia. Maybe a 'Yoda meets the natural world'? But it will combine entertainment and drama with revelation and breakthrough in science as we enter their world, I hope.

Dan Brockington
Reader in Environment and Development
University of Manchester

Advisor to:
A Place without People
Unnatural Histories: The Serengeti
Conservation's Dirty Secrets

I belong to a small group of academics whose subject of enquiry is the wildlife film industry itself. Authors like Greg Mitman (*Reel Nature*) and Derek Bousé (*Wildlife Films*) have produced fascinating books whose main topic was the history of the industry and its different genres. I come from a slightly different perspective: my interest in the wildlife film industry is its relationship to the environmental and conservation movements. One of the unnoticed facts about modern environmental movements is that their proliferation coincides with wildlife film. The mass audiences of the BBC, David Attenborough's career and the WWF have similar start dates; in some respects they have co-evolved. Environmentalism and conservation are televised movements and without considering the influence of wildlife film on them our understanding of them will be poorer.

I am a newcomer, beginning work on this topic only in 2006 and attending my first Wildscreen in 2008. However the wildlife film-making community is a thoughtful and reflective one. This makes exploring interactions between conservation impact and film rewarding.

The relationship between wildlife film and conservation can be surprisingly ambivalent. This is strange because wildlife film-makers are really good at making awe-inspiring films which stir people's hearts with a love for nature. Many conservationists would count watching beautiful wildlife films as among the experiences that inspired them to become better naturalists. Furthermore, as Alan Root observed, the making of a wildlife film can require a good deal of bushcraft, an intimacy with the wild on which conservation movements have long hinged.

But treating people to beautiful sights, or titillating them with never-before-seen shots of rare wildlife doing unusual things to each other does not necessarily serve the conservation movement well. The primary goal of such films is entertainment. It is about keeping the audience amused, enthralled and above all, watching. It is much less interested in getting them to act, protest, or change their behaviour, which is what effective conservation often requires.

In that respect conservation has been quite unwelcome to film commissioners. Conservation is about difficult issues of change, loss and awkward politics. It is not what you want to sit down to after a hard day's work. Most of the public watch television to relax, not to be challenged. Furthermore conservation issues tend to be presented in rather worthy ways, by rather worthy people, which are most off-putting to peak-time audiences. The political issues rapidly become dated, and rarely travel well to international audiences, and this matters if you want to make a film that could be repeatedly shown on National Geographic. Orangutans, preferably fighting or mating, have a timeless appeal all over the world; orangutans dying among the palm oil plantations that have invaded their territory do not. Putting conservation into a pitch could put off the commissioners.

I understand that some of the Wildscreen festivals in the 1990s – during the heyday of the blue-chip film days and the boom of the industry – had relatively little to say about conservation. The film-makers' job was to make beautiful inspiring films, and the conservationists' was to turn the audiences into activists by other

189

means. But not all film-makers are satisfied with this sort of situation. They want their films to make a difference, they love the threatened nature they are privileged to see, and they do not want to live as parasites returning so little directly to the world which nurtured them. Part of the reason why organisations like Filmmakers for Conservation was founded is because of a dissatisfaction with the conservation impact of wildlife film-making compared with what could be achieved.

But this state of affairs is hard to discern from the tone of recent Wildscreen festivals, for these have been dominated by environmentalist and conservation sentiment. The commercial logics described above remain (and hence in 2008 the commissioner for Channel 5 did simply say 'no conservation' when outlining her interests), but the moral imperative, the call to serve conservation causes, is far stronger and clearer than before. There is a realization, too, among film-makers that conservation messages can be made into good entertaining film. In the words of one commissioner at Wildscreen 2010, 'Perhaps conservation is not a dirty word anymore'.

The change is symbolised by the award of the Golden Panda in 2010 to the extraordinary film *Green*. Hard-hitting films have won the Golden Panda before (such as those by Mike Pandey) but *Green* broke all the normal rules about wildlife film-making. It was about the forest destruction in Indonesia and the orangutans dying among its oil plantations. It told a complex story about the commodity chains that implicate our lives in those catastrophes. Moreover it did so in a forty-minute film that contained *one word* of narration and no musical score for the first fifteen minutes. And if that is not enough, the runner, researcher, cameraman, producer and director, Patrick Rouxel, who was (almost) solely responsible for *Green*'s existence, then made it freely available on the web for anyone to download.

So what do the coming years portend for the relationship between conservation and wildlife film? I can see some changes in the offing, a potential radical change that may follow it, and one strong continuity. The obvious development, now unfolding, is that conservation and environmentalist issues are being turned into good entertaining films. There are several reasons for this. In part it is because we need new stories about the places film-makers know. One BBC researcher at Wildscreen 2010 opined that 'Africa has already been filmed', meaning that the standard representations of Africa found in many wildlife films are becoming rather familiar. There is also dissatisfaction with current emotive engagements. One experienced observer at Wildscreen 2010 contended that sometimes the only emotional register he could see in wildlife film was awe. That is a problem. It will not work in a cable environment with fractured audiences demanding a multitude of emotional experiences.

Also it is because of the success of genres like *Springwatch*, whose popularity hinges on audience participation and the sort of active engagement on which conservation thrives. Furthermore it is because the technological transformations of Web 2.0 allow far more audience engagement, and because audiences demand it. Finally it is because there are so many interesting stories to tell and film-makers are getting better at finding new ways of telling them. Conservation is not necessarily worthy. It can be fun, and entertaining television.

It is possible, therefore, that the notoriously conservative commissioners will become increasingly receptive to the possibilities conservation film offers. The bigger challenge, the radical possibility beyond that, is that film-makers could begin to engage critically with conservation itself in ways that do not represent it simply as the solution to environmental problems, but in some cases as the cause of other problems. This is a hard ask with a complicated message. But the potential for fascinating storylines here is great. The murkier world of conservation includes rural people who insist they are enemies of conservation, and extractive industries who have become its friends; it includes indigenous identities invented and transformed both for and against conservation purposes; it includes false degradation narratives and tragic injustice sustained and nurtured, unwittingly, by the great and the good.

The continuity is that, in the midst of all the commercial pressure and changes described above, we must remember that there is a long tradition of influential conservation film. Such films rarely sustain production companies; they may not even be popular, but then they are not intended to be. There exists a small but significant undercurrent of powerful conservation films that are aimed at tiny audiences (the boards of important companies, ministers making decisions about habitat destruction or wildlife trade) that have had far-reaching consequences. These are not well-known stories; their successes are often secret. But when the power of the medium and the skill of its messengers are concentrated on so few people then the results can, and will, be dramatic.

Richard Brock
Executive Producer
Living Planet Productions & The Brock Initiative

Freshly Squeezed Giraffe
Volesville
The Egret has Landed

From general assistant and radio, to executive producer for global television, in the BBC Natural History Unit for thirty-five years. The best bits? *Life on Earth* and *The Living Planet* because of their impact and their reach. The worst? Realising that what was happening to the natural world was not being transmitted to the television audience. How could the biggest broadcasting organisation on the planet continue effectively to lie about our impact on our only home?

Not only was it a continuing lie, getting more serious as the deceit hid the problems, but if anybody had the strength to tell the truth (and maybe lose some viewers?) it was the BBC. It simply didn't have the guts. So, misleading, glossy programmes on jungles appeared on BBC1 and four million viewers got no perspective on their situation anywhere. Those programmes that did tell the truth about such matters went to BBC4, with its four viewers who already knew what was happening.

Famously, *The Blue Planet* series was shown on BBC1, except for the last programme called *Deep Trouble*, which was transmitted on BBC2, so millions were misled on BBC1 and the relatively few, who knew, got the truth on 2. On Discovery, in the US, they didn't even show the last programme. At a big fund-raising event for the marine enviroment, a potential donor was approached: he said he'd seen the *The Blue Planet* series and thought there were no problems to be paid for. A disservice.

Then, certainly bigger, came *Planet Earth*. But was it better? Some thought not, like respected TV critic of the Sunday Times (circulation

1.2m) AA Gill: "The BBC has become so practised at these vast, soft-centred über-nature films that there's a sort of vain swagger to them. The beautiful images come on with the flourish of Italian opera, confident and patronising in their ability to astonish. After ten minutes of all this wonder and skill and sublime bloody panoramic beauty, I simply couldn't take any more. I'd come to the end of the godlike, hyper-real, grand-production nature series. I've had the box set, the tea-tray books, the repeats. That's it. The genre has collapsed under its own self-regard and become a parody of itself. Let me just tell you a few of the things that choked me last Sunday. First it was poor old David Attenborough, who's become the Laurence Olivier of voice-overs, the stand-in voice of God. You could hear the resignation, the swallowed disgust at the copious streams of fruity, clichéd, sentimental bilge he had to intone like Christmas-card greetings over the film. The factual content is now virtually nil, just scene-setting and needless telling you what you're seeing. There was barely any attempt to differentiate between North and South Poles. Who cared? And the observation becomes ever more disengaged from a human-sized reality. The camera angles get higher and wider, giving an omnipotent view, and the sentimentally grandiose music is beyond bearing, like the overblown accompaniment to a silent movie or Tchaikovsky orchestrating cartoons. The wildlife itself is sentimentalised, anthropomorphised and edited into a cute narrative in a way I thought we'd all grown out of with Disney in the 1950s. But mostly what I mind is the hidden hand of American culture and scientific social censorship. Like most big BBC nature series, this was a co-production with the Discovery channel, which has a long and weird set of requirements for its products: very little violence, no blood, hardly any sex and very, very hazy, non-committal science, especially where it may contentiously upset fundamental Christians. Essentially what it wants is pretty, unnatural nature for ten-year-old, conservative Midwestern creationists. Now, I understand that this sort of programme is eye-wateringly expensive, and getting other broadcasters to share the expense makes bottom-line sense. But the BBC is not a commercial company: your licence fee is being used to subsidise American commercial television, and it's being made to their specifications. The BBC is the world's biggest broadcaster. Only it has the experience and the ability to make programmes of this stature. And it can sell them around the world after they're made. It shouldn't sell them before. This is our television, not a bespoke nature tailor for America. The interference, both overt and unstated, in the BBC's programming should be a central question in the renewal of the licence fee. It is one of the most damaging interventions in our culture. British television is in danger of going the way of British film: becoming a source of highly skilled technicians hired out to make someone else's culture." !!

193

Of course great blue-chip television gets interest, perhaps concern, and not every programme has to have a strident sermon attached to it. Today, eventually, these issues are up front, often cleverly presented, but is it in time? For the future, television has had its chance. Perhaps my past frustration will lead to new worlds of communication, vital to life on earth.

I left the BBC Natural History Unit in July 1995 with many happy memories, from bat caves with a film crew and David Attenborough to seeing some of the most extraordinary frogs anyone could imagine doing, the most impossible things. I'm not sure that today those caves or frogs are as they were. What I do know is that they need all the help they can get in a world where endless material growth seems as desirable as it is unattainable. To turn that round is a massive challenge – look at Brazil, India and China, where population growth and consumerism are a deadly combination. But with this so-called progress are, indeed, some benefits that might just get results in time – as television becomes less and less of a player in this reach for eyes, ears and minds. It might even reach politicians!

In the meantime, it seems to me, wildlife television plods on. How much snuff and fang TV can we take? Can Discovery and National Geographic go on producing snuff stuff like *Killer Elephants* or *Killed by Coyotes*, where young viewers see endless "fearsome predators", yet more "murderous", "deadly", "ruthless", sharks, bears, tigers, when the real threats to us are CO_2 and HIV? No wonder they may grow up to regard wildlife as aggressive, dangerous and to-be-got-rid-of. Cue yet more clones of wrangling heroes. How depressing.

In time, I believe these audience-hungry, worn-out themes will look even more dated than they do now. The expensive blue-chips, sons of *Planet Earth* & Co., will themselves become an endangered species. Yet, I suppose there are new viewers who have not seen the Serengeti migration with those fearsome predators, the crocodiles, or bears fishing for salmon. Now, the real question is the proposed road across the Serengeti, or climate change in Alaska and why it's really China's fault, burning all that coal. To me these true wonders of nature are more interesting, certainly more important because of the perspective we can now put on them.

David Attenborough and *State of the Planet* eventually told us the truth in a big way. Festivals seem to have been ahead of the broadcasters. Top world awards went to Hugh Miles and his team for *People of the Sea*, revealing the mismanagement of Canadian fisheries, with superb wildlife footage and an intriguing story. They went where *The Blue Planet* feared to tread, although the legendary Jacques Cousteau had been warning us about the threat to the oceans with his French-poetic philosophies. *Green*, from Patrick Rouxel, also from France, won the Golden Panda at Wildscreen 2010 with a wordless tragedy leading to the death of a female orangutan, caused by our demand for shampoo and much else, via palm oil. And Bernard Walton, one of my previous team-mates at the BBC, won well with his film about the restoration of the Iraq marshes, without a fearsome predator in sight – unless you include a rare reed warbler that eats insects – only, from the past, Saddam Hussein, an extreme version of the dangerous human animal we are.

Meanwhile I had made over forty films with Living Planet Productions distributed to forty countries. They were all conservation stories and I like to think they made a difference – and maybe still do? We are now listing films and film-makers that have really made a difference, to encourage others and show the way:

www.filmmakersforconservation.org/conservation-filmmaking/film-library.html

It's not easy to prove, but today, if a big issue has been aired and the situation improved, then surely global television (and more) must have been partly responsible? For BBC1 we made a film about the last female wolf in Sweden, killed in that civilised country. People complained to the Swedish embassy and boycotted Volvo cars. Today Sweden makes room for some hundred wolves, Norway hardly any. But wolves are now doing well all over Europe, and are not seen these days so much as fearsome predators – despite Little Red Riding Hood and National Geographic.

Today television has less impact. But Discovery's *Whale Wars* is exciting drama on the high seas that, eventually, may help stop whaling. *Lost Land of the Tiger* claimed to be pioneering, but wasn't, and by identifying locations provided a super sat-nav for Chinese poachers in Bhutan. They gave copies of the films to the government, but what is really needed is specific short versions for local use, from top to bottom of society, for all ages, in whatever language and style is appropriate. Compared with the series budget for helicopters, for example, this would cost peanuts, could use trainee film-makers and really help the tigers of Bhutan. At present, five million viewers on their sofas in Britain can make very little difference to the reality in the Himalayas.

195

The Brock Initiative has evolved a formula to reach out and make a difference. We write three lists:

1. Whom do you need to reach? Who's involved with the issue? "The Stakeholders"? From president to young child.
2. What films would you make for each audience? Test them out before finishing and get the audience involved so they come to share the project and be proud of it.
3. List the various considerations of equipment, from local cinema to mobile phone. Often films are shown, but miss their potential. A school-room crammed with excited African kids may seem to have been a successful event: but actually only the front few rows could see it, and the sound went nowhere.

This formula has been used worldwide, more recently in Kenya to save that rare antelope, the Mountain Bongo. To see so many schools around the endangered forests run 'Bongo Clubs' with so much enthusiasm is so encouraging compared with the remote indifference of a typical British television audience. To me there is no question where the job is better done. And much more cheaply too. The children will pass the message on. Many have a mobile phone in their mud hut. The schools have the internet, and it's from these newer technologies that differences will surely be made.

And there's more: two major changes are involved. In the last ten years, public interest in, and concern for, the environment has increased to reach every country and most people. Supermarkets have become "green in tooth and claw". Climate change is everywhere. How nigh, in fact, is the end of the world? At the same time the explosion of communication has spread everywhere too, the latest fashion being Twitter, Facebook, YouTube and hundreds of other networks, and surely it's just the beginning. Some is bound to be rubbish but some is bound, I say, to save bongos, bluefin tuna, turtles and a lake in Kenya. Now, with what I call "Filming with Attitude", using modest equipment, low-profile and accurate reporting, the world has the chance to show itself what's going wrong – and to suggest solutions.

Waitrose has lied about importing so-called "sustainable" (not) flowers from Lake Naivasha. Then they had the chance to put that right by funding a scientifically-researched plan and advertise the fact in competition with the other big supermarkets. Despite the huge profits they shout about, they continue to harm a beautiful lake of rare freshwater in Kenya, claiming "Whatever we touch we aim to make better". For Valentine's and Mother's days The Brock Initiative's press release, that went worldwide, was "Please your Mother, Kill a Lake". That's the real price of a rose and now lots of people know.

Mitsubishi is a Japanese industrial giant: cars and chemicals. Not fish. But it decided to buy up as much bluefin tuna as it could before stocks ran out. Like gold, the rarer the tuna gets, the richer Mitsubishi gets, until this immensely valuable resource for the world's people is extinct. How greedy and selfish is that? Expensive restaurants refuse to ban it. Celebrities are embroiled. Lots of publicity, mostly bad for Mitsubishi, featured in the movie *End of the Line*. So they gave some money to the Wildfowl and Wetland Trust (WWT) to save the world's rarest duck: the Madagascar Pochard. Not a fish, a duck. Is that greenwash?

Now WWT is taking money from massive Cargill, accused of destroying the Amazon for beef, soya and sugar. "We are eating the Amazon", a leading rainforest scientist says in my film.

Mitsubishi has a new electric car: the i-MiEV. So has Nissan, and most of the others. Soon the internet will suggest you don't buy Mitsubishis as they are knowingly and single-mindedly causing the extinction of a magnificent ocean creature, known because of its speed and value as the "Porsche of the Sea": the bluefin tuna.

In Turkey, sea turtles are in trouble. Despite using one as its logo, Hilton Hotels is not helping; TUI, the huge German tour company, denies guilt; and First Choice may become an internet-user's last choice when it comes to choosing a holiday on one of their beaches. Illegal building, water sports, lights and music at night have reduced the breeding population of turtles, where unsuspecting tourists had no idea of the damage being done. They do now. And they and others may choose differently next time – if there is one. Footage of this bad behaviour, based on careful studies, has gone round the world and to the European legal process. The Turkish government is under pressure. More filming will follow to check on any change, good and bad, and expose it. That footage will be seen by web-followers, some of the very customers those hotels and that country depend on for income. There will be nowhere to hide.

For example, in 2011, as reported by Claire Beale in *The Independent*:
"VW is the latest blue-chip brand to be targeted by Greenpeace, and the result is a brilliant pastiche of a VW campaign launched at this year's Super Bowl ... went on to score well over forty million views on YouTube. ... Greenpeace urges us to sign up to the rebellion against VW's record on carbon dioxide emissions. The spoof has been an

197

instant success, generating millions of pounds'-worth of publicity and creating an internet firestorm that has left Volkswagen reeling. ... Last year Greenpeace turned its fire on Nestlé, with an ad that showed an office worker crunching on an orangutan's finger as if it was a Kit Kat. The campaign attacked Nestlé's relationship with the Indonesian palm oil producer Sinar Mas, which Greenpeace has accused of illegal deforestation. The beauty of Greenpeace's approach is that it uses all the familiarity and brand awareness that its victims have spent millions of advertising pounds to build, and turns that against the brands themselves. It could teach plenty of bigger-budgeted companies a thing or two about communications."

This is really power to the (conservation) people. Large companies are not used to being leaned on like this. They talk a lot about Corporate Social Responsibility (CSR). Now the proof is on the internet everywhere for everyone, and it can come from anyone who cares, gets their facts right and can pick up a camera, a mobile phone or one of the many clever gadgets that can take pictures and deliver them. If this spreads, as it is doing, old-style TV, new-style HD and 3D and Disney Nature in the cinemas will be merely add-ons. Not only will they be about dinosaurs, they will become dinosaurs. Yet the content, be it a tiny wren or a giant pterodactyl, will continue to intrigue and excite. Whether it's shot on super 4D IMAX with knobs on, or cardboard, won't matter if it reaches people and affects them.

Compared with the old days of five-man wildlife film crews, thirty pieces of luggage, a fixture in the BBC schedules of national importance, we now have almost the opposite: one amateur person, one gadget, and, say, YouTube. If that continues, as I believe it could, the natural world must surely become a better place. I certainly hope so.

Mat Thompson
Wildlife Cameraman / Producer
Freelance

The Wild Side Of London – Passion Wild (Passion Pictures)
Flight of Butterflies (SK Films)
Hudson's Monarch (Winner BBC Newcomer Wildscreen 2010 – Self Produced)

After graduating I started my working career in creative marketing. A life-long naturalist and self-confessed wildlife film geek, I realised working with the natural world was my true calling and that my creative ideas and artistic eye could be used well within the wildlife film industry. My goal became to work on the some of the programmes I had grown up adoring. Step forward five years: I found myself picking up the BBC Newcomer Award at Wildscreen 2010, selling material to the NHU, shooting and developing stories for a BBC *Natural World* under a fantastic director, and running into folks like Chris Packham, Doug Allen and many others. It's been a great journey so far!

It's hard for me to talk about how the industry has changed from an insider's perspective as I haven't known it for that long. However, writing this at the end of a two-month project in Colorado, and having watched a lot of Animal Planet in the US over this time, a few things do come to mind. Fangs, claws, killer-this and killer-that! A large portion of the airtime seems to be filled with programming based on the quick fix of YouTube 'hit culture'. I have seen very little in the way of great storytelling and informative, creative, beautiful natural history.

I'd like to see broadcasters commissioning more films based on solid stories and creative formatting with positive conservation messages. Short format would, in my opinion, also make our natural history viewing more diverse and give the independent film-maker more chance to get their work commissioned and/or broadcast. This also fits with modern viewing trends: content that's short, digestible and creatively conceived. The BBC used to run a ten-minute short film strand that I personally thought was great. I'd love to see these types of strands sewn into our mainstream viewing on a more regular basis. At the other end of the scale, the last few years have seen the emergence of cinematic, feature-length wildlife releases and of course 3D. More of these are now in production and I'm sure they will continue to grow into a great platform for epic big-budget films. I feel that 3D certainly has its unique place and, for wildlife films, has considerable value. Wildlife films, after all, can be an escape, and a 3D cinema screen is certainly an immersive situation. I just hope its future use will be based on solid storytelling, rather than its becoming a theme park attraction.

For a budding film-maker, camera technology over recent years has made it easier and easier to produce fabulous imagery. This takes nothing away from the skills involved in making a good film, of course. But it certainly means that, financially, great imagery is within the grasp of many more people. Even throughout the two years of making my film *Hudson's Monarch* the game was changing. DSLR video emerged and, although maybe not the panacea many heralded, it does enable fantastic imagery to be produced at staggeringly low prices. This and other technology is certain to be refined and get cheaper. While the boundaries of what is top-shelf natural history imaging will also get pushed higher, I believe that in the coming years we will see true broadcast and cinematic cameras available for prices that many can afford. This will certainly give great potential for new independent producers to produce high-quality work that is less bound by financial constraint.

So what advice could I give to existing and future wildlife film-makers? Well my success so far has come simply from doing what I love: dreaming up ideas, picking up a camera and producing films as best as I can. I know a number of people who hold good positions within the industry who have told me they wish they had tried for an award such as the BBC Newcomer. I'm always a little surprised they haven't been driven to do so already, by the same desire that got them into the industry in the first place. The pre-conceived need for exotic locations or 'A-list' animals is certainly part of this. But to the budding wildlife film-maker I'd say, do yourself a favour, keep it local. There is plenty of untapped material waiting to be shot, plenty of characters waiting to be discovered, plenty of stories waiting to be told, and all right on your doorstep.

So I guess I would simply suggest that anyone trying to enter this industry starts making their own films and gets them out into public forums. Let's face it: in today's online world it's now easier than it has ever been. By getting your own films out there you'll begin to meet like-minded people and build relationships and ideas. Entering film festivals is also a sure-fire way to get yourself exposure and build contacts. What I'd also add: involve yourself in other non-film-making wildlife groups. I have volunteered at a wildlife hospital for a few years, been part of nest-recording groups and helped at nature reserves. With this comes not only the pleasure of getting out and getting close to the wildlife we all love, but it also starts to show you the sorts of characters, places and animals that make up many wildlife programmes. I'm sure that before very long you'll start coming across great ideas and stories, and of course have some great fun on the way!

Alex Rhodes
15 Year-Old Aspiring Wildlife Film-maker
Bristol Grammar School

I'm a young person determined to pursue a career in wildlife and conservation film-making, and have been a wildlife watcher all my life. I'm fascinated by documenting the natural world and the many, varied events that occur within it, and have been since I was young. At thirteen, I used the family's DSLR to shoot wildlife. At fourteen, I borrowed my neighbour's Sony PD150P and busied myself building natural hides in the local woodland. At fifteen, I was given a proper hide – not just a flimsy contraption made from a few bits of rotting wood and leaves. My contribution here is to give a novice's input about how the wildlife film industry looks from my position, revering the Doug Allans and David Attenboroughs I grew up watching. At the time of writing, I have no credits to my name, but enough ambitions to entertain me for the rest of my life!

I'm a child of the digital age. I have no experience of scratching a

201

precious vinyl with the needle, mixing the wrong chemicals in a darkroom when developing negatives, or having to double-check my exposure calculation when using a flash. Instead I hit the motor drive as hard as I like and simply delete any poor images at the touch of a button. I've had a camera since I was at nursery school and have always been encouraged to explore technology. Life has been predominantly digital for me – using the family DSLR and borrowing my kind neighbour's camcorder!

In my lifetime, albeit short, I have seen the transition from VHS to DVD and Blue-ray disc. Other changes that have great potential include the integration of HD video into DSLRs. On finding our old handheld HDV camcorder recently, I was surprised to find a huge memory stick inserted in it with the minute capacity of only 25 MB. In contrast, it's incredible to think of the fingernail-sized 64 GB memory card or the low cost of a 2 TB hard drive you can purchase today – things have come a long way in just a decade! It does, however, strongly affect my plans and future outlook. I'm saving up to invest in my own HD kit, far from the £60k+ pro-spec kit of the BBC, but still a considerable amount for someone my age to amass. The trouble is I can splash out on the latest gadgetry, and within two years know it will be replaced by a new all-singing-all-dancing model with extra flashing lights and gizmos! I shall have to think long and hard about both the economics and lifespan of any product I do buy and aim to find something that will do me well for the next period of my career.

Right now, HD or High Definition is the big thing. It has become, with a few odd exceptions, the industry standard for broadcasting, and most blue-chips are shot on HD. I think in ten years' time HD *will* be the base format, and that you will be hard pushed to broadcast or even find any Standard Definition (SD) materials at all. Indeed, for the majority of television broadcasting companies, the minimum requirement for submitting material is HD and they will not accept anything less. So then you ask yourself, well what is the next step forward? I know people have mixed feelings about 3D imagery – personally I like it. It's funky and can be used advantageously to bring the viewer right into the action. But most of the time, however, I feel it's best to leave 3D imagery to short, specially commissioned productions where the main aim is entertainment, and not education. I would find it somewhat disheartening if the BBC NHU suddenly shot all their blue-chips on 3D – I feel it would somehow lower their distinctive calibre and the BBC would lose their distinguished, idiosyncratic status in the world of wildlife film. I'm not saying that 3D should be abandoned – it's a great way to get the public engaged – but currently to shoot something fully on 3D you need an awful lot of funding, and a specialised workforce to handle it. As with all technologies, doubtless, Moore's Law will prevail, and 3D cameras will be as compact, lightweight, accessible and flexible as today's handheld video equivalents. Perhaps a decade isn't long enough for the evolution of 3D imagery: I've had mixed responses from the people I've spoken to. Perhaps it will need twenty or thirty years to replace HD entirely, or perhaps it will fade and then have a resurgence. Another change I foresee is that more film documentary emphasis will go on the pressing aspects of climate change, biodiversity loss and conservation. A friend of mine told me that wildlife photographers are having a hard time right now: their stuff just isn't selling. Picture libraries are more interested in photographers who can document global issues and human interaction with nature, as these are selling better than pure natural history. Media focus will be on the delicate balance and relationships within our planet.

I believe there is a market for productions that engage and encourage the viewer to explore the natural world and love the outdoors. Just look at the audiences *Springwatch* and *Autumnwatch* get, and how this has increased in the past few years. I suspect we shall see a rapid rise in the type of programmes and documentaries that set off the spark and make the public further want to explore, understand and be captivated by the natural world, wanting to conserve wildlife and make a difference to their planet. After all, isn't this one of the main aims of wildlife and conservation film-makers/photographers? The same is true with the education of youngsters. They are the next generation of caretakers, destined to inherit the earth. Eventually, what *they* do will dictate how the natural world will fare – it is up to us to educate them properly to make responsible decisions. So more focus will need to go on the productions that influence the way young people think and act towards nature.

While many of us aspiring film-makers and camera operators long to get our hands on a full HD camcorder with a huge telephoto lens and a whacking great tripod to stabilise it all, it is easy to waste so much time surfing for kit – only to be disappointed by the price tag. I'll own up: that's what I did for a long period of time, and I fully regret the time I wasted. GET WHAT YOU CAN AND USE IT! I currently borrow an SD camcorder off a kind neighbour. It's an old, well-used Sony PD150P with which I practise all the skills I can – smooth pans, focus pulling etc. The more experience you get, the greater the chance someone will notice you. So what if none of your material will ever be broadcast? At least I can now successfully follow a swallow in flight, albeit my efforts are with a 12x zoom lens. I have learned the skill and hand-work to do

203

it. When my time comes, and I do finally get my hands on a 40x lens, I will be better at keeping track with the birds than the person who has spent the last however many years looking at the internet, making a wish list and not doing anything!

My second piece of advice is to network. I know you will have heard this from others, but I can't emphasis just how useful and effective it is to get yourself known! You need to have courage though, to keep pushing yourself. Don't expect to be noticed immediately – most people won't remember 'the last time we met', but occasionally one or two will greet you (to your surprise) and remember the impression you left on them last time. Keep prompting your name, details, what you want from them, how they know you – and soon it will sink in. And on that point, don't be afraid to let them know how much you really admire their work or style of presentation – it will show your awareness and help them to remember you. Get them to critique your work – whether it is for still images or short clips of interesting behaviour. Find out what they like about it, and how you could improve ... then do it! Explore new techniques and push your creativity past your comfortable boundaries – out of the many failures, there will be something new, quite different from anything else done before, that someone, somewhere in the world, will like.

After all, you can only get better!

204

Conclusions

First of all, a huge thank you to all the contributors for taking time to share their passion and predictions in this book. You have read about a wide range of career paths, experiences and hopes and visions for the future of the wildlife film-making industry. Along the way a number of key points has arisen, in many of the contributions, which we shall now summarise:

High Definition: the development of HD technology, solid-state recording, and the continuing fall in the cost of memory, have all made the acquisition of high-quality images available to an increasing number of people, even those on relatively low budgets. Many of these technological advances have been explored in more detail in the chapter, *Changes in Technology*. Broadcasters, increasingly, will accept only HD now. More people making films with high-quality images means more competition, but that doesn't mean they will all be good films.

New audiences: the number of ways you can reach an audience is increasing. As well as television there is the internet, web-channels such as YouTube, phone/tablet applications, interactive displays for installations and so on. How some of these opportunities will make money (for the production) is still unclear and under debate. As television and the internet converge we shall maybe see pay-per-view as a common protocol. The challenge, as more people make films that are available in more ways, is how to reach your audience: how to let them know your film is there, and worth watching.

Multi-tasking: it is increasingly unlikely that you will have a job that requires you to perform just one operation (eg editing or research). In the future you will find yourself involved in various tasks required to complete a film, whatever your nominal role.

Multi-skilling: associated with multi-tasking is the fact that you are more likely to succeed if you have a multitude of skills. Even if your aim is, for example, to become principally a wildlife camera operator, it is certain to help if you are also able to edit video, record sound, deal with digital files, create websites etc. It may help if you can also present and/or narrate. This multi-skilling can be extended, especially if you are just starting out, to many other ways you could be of use to a film crew (and to yourself): cooking, vehicle maintenance, hide/platform-building, scuba-diving, navigation and so on. It is also strongly recommended that you acquire a good working knowledge of computer programs such as Word, Excel, Photoshop, and a good website-building tool such as Dreamweaver. There will always be a need for specialists, of course, but the more skills you have, the more use you will be in any situation, the more employable you become, and the less you will need to rely on (and pay for) others.

Changing styles: the future of classic, behavioural, blue-chip wildlife films is, as ever, up for debate. But numerous contributors have predicted that we are likely to see fewer big-budget observational films and more human-animal interaction programmes (see also *conservation content* discussed below).

3D: the jury is out! Some love it, some think it a passing fad. Whatever your view, we shall certainly see more 3D (and beyond!) productions in the future.

Storytelling: as the battle for audiences rages on, and with it the desire for excellence in film-making, it is clear from many of our contributors that the art of storytelling is key to many successful films. Too often an afterthought, or lost in the race to use new technology, a strong, engaging story can make the difference between an award-winning, memorable event and a forgettable visual experience. Producers with a strong sense of story, and professional scriptwriters, will (or should) always be priorities in the team.

Make films: with a budget HD camcorder, and a laptop with an editing program (even the free ones that come with computers, such as Movie Maker or iMovie), it is more affordable than ever to make your own films. Most of our writers agree this is a great way to learn the craft – give it a go – just do it!

Conservation content: when the organisation Filmmakers for Conservation was formed in 2000, there was very little conservation at all on television. And indeed, that short time ago, the majority of the general public knew little of topics such as climate change. Much has changed since then. Few people in the 'developed' world have not heard of global warming now, and there are conservation aspects to more productions than previously. While this seems like a step in the right direction, we have to ask ourselves if film-makers could be doing more in this regard. The sad state of affairs is currently that, although steps to reduce global warming are being taken, they are too little and too late compared to the amount of irreversible climate change we are on the brink of experiencing.

Although there are many different environmental problems throughout the world, and many different organisations each trying to do their own focussed bit of good, the fact that we hadn't quite grasped ten years ago is that climate change is poised to eclipse all of these. The forecast storms, droughts, floods, mass extinctions, oil-, food-, land- and water-wars etc would change our world and the wildlife within it in ways that are almost impossible to comprehend. A poll of adults in the UK last year showed that the number of people who are sceptical about climate change is rising worryingly; the media inevitably have a large part to play in this. Whether it is the job of the *wildlife* film-maker to do anything about this is a matter of opinion, but, as you have read, the passion of people who want to use film to 'make a difference' is hotter than ever. It could be argued that this is the job of a different breed of film-maker – the environmental documentary-maker – rather than the true wildlife film-maker whose speciality is recording the wonder and beauty of the natural history of this planet: but inevitably there is much crossover.

Whatever your view in this regard, the sobering fact is that if climate change continues unchecked, much of the wildlife we are now filming will not exist in the future as it does now. We can either resign ourselves to documenting this biodiversity in its last few decades, or join the fight to raise awareness and limit damage, whether this is part of our film-making or not.

The future of the planet and its natural history may not be looking too bright right now, but the future of wildlife film-making and the passionate individuals who forge the craft shines on.

Further Reading

Wild Pages: The Wildlife Film-makers Resource Guide edited by
Jason Peters and Piers Warren – published by Wildeye 2011

A complete tool-kit of information for all wildlife film-makers – established and newcomers. Listings of wildlife production companies, footage libraries, distributors, broadcasters, location managers / fixers, film festivals, organisations, publications and more, with contact details, weblinks and descriptions. Including answers to those all-important questions such as whether they take people on work experience or consider co-productions, how to submit proposals etc. Invaluable information at your fingertips to save hours of trawling through the Internet and sending many emails.
(see www.wildeye.co.uk/shop.html)

Careers in Wildlife Film-making by Piers Warren – published by
Wildeye 2002, 2006

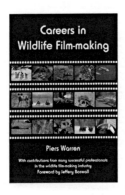

The essential book by Piers Warren, packed with guidance and advice for aspiring makers of natural history films. Described as 'long-overdue' and 'much-needed', this is not just an essential book for newcomers and wannabes - the fascinating case studies of well-known individuals, and unique discussion of the future of the industry from top professionals, make this an important read for those already working in the fields of wildlife, underwater and conservation film.
(see www.wildeye.co.uk/shop.html)

Go Wild with your Camcorder - How to Make Wildlife Films by Piers Warren – published by Wildeye 2006

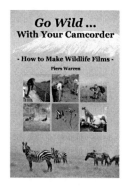

Whether you want to film wildlife as a fascinating hobby, or are hoping for a career as a professional wildlife film-maker, this book and a basic camcorder are all you need to get started! Packed with information and advice acquired over years of teaching wildlife film-making Piers Warren guides you through all aspects of making a wildlife film from choosing a camcorder to editing the final product.
(see www.wildeye.co.uk/shop.html)

Shooting in the Wild: An Insider's Account of Making Movies in the Animal Kingdom by Chris Palmer – published by Sierra Club Books 2010

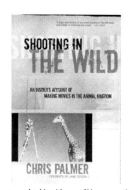

Longtime producer Chris Palmer provides an in-depth look at wild animals on film, covering the history of wildlife documentaries, safety issues, and the never-ending pressure to obtain the "money shot." Marlin Perkins, Jacques Cousteau, Steve Irwin, Timothy Treadwell, and many other familiar names are discussed along with their work, accidents, and in some cases, untimely deaths. Chris Palmer is highly critical of Irwin, and offers fascinating revelations about game farms used by exploitative filmmakers and photographers looking for easy shots and willing to use caged animals to obtain them. He also considers the subliminal messages of many wildlife films, considering everything from *Shark Week* to *Happy Feet* and how they manipulate audiences toward preset conclusions about animal behavior. In all this is an engaging and exceedingly timely look at a form of entertainment the public has long taken for granted and which, as Chris Palmer points out, really needs a fresh and careful reconsideration.

Africa's Big Five And Other Wildlife Film Makers by Jean Hartley – published by Twaweza Communications 2010

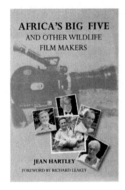

Jean Hartley, born in Kenya, is acknowledged as being the first to legitimise "fixing" for wildlife film crews. Over the last 25 years, she has worked on over a thousand films, the vast majority being about wildlife and nature. In this insightful book she features five of the great film-makers who all started their careers in Kenya in the 1950s, legends whom she is proud to call personal friends. Watching all their films, and many more, she became fascinated by the history of film-making in Kenya and determined to find out when it all started. She traces the roots of wildlife film back a hundred years, drawing on accounts of the original film makers and the professional hunters who guided those early safaris. She tracks the changes from those grainy, speeded up, silent films through to the technologically perfect High Definition and 3D films that are being made today. (see www.wildeye.co.uk/shop.html)

Wildlife Films by Derek Bousé – published by University of Pennsylvania Press 2000

This book is a scholarly analysis of the development of wildlife films up to the 21st century. Derek Bousé's exploration of wildlife film-making over the last few hundred years is fascinating, and the book is littered with behind-the-scenes anecdotes. Although the book focuses on the industry in the USA and UK, the discussions (to what extent are wildlife films documentaries for example) are applicable to wildlife film-makers the world over. There are so many well-known names – both companies and individuals – in the business today, and it's hard to keep track as units change name, merge or disappear. This book certainly helps piece the jigsaw together as the genre's development is analysed.

100 Years of Wildlife by Michael Bright – published by BBC Books 2007

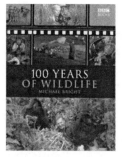

Ever since 1907, when a flickering film about birds enthralled a cinema audience, we've been fascinated by watching the natural world on film. For 100 years wildlife films have taken us to places and shown us things we would never be able to see – the excitement, the strangeness, the danger of the wild. Today, our interest in the wonders of the natural world is stronger than ever. Discover the history of the wildlife moving image: the first heady days when an ant juggling a matchbox was big box office; the charismatic and sometimes controversial celebrity presenters; the astonishing behaviour of animals and plants; the boggling oddities of nature; the animals now extinct that poignantly only exist on film. Explore 100 years of revelation – from the black-and-white silent footage that started it all to the almost magical photography techniques seen today in programmes like *Planet Earth*. From famous faces of wildlife TV to extraordinary animal (and plant) behaviour, natural history filming has changed the way we look at and think about our world. It's all here – so weird, you couldn't make it up; so wonderful, you wouldn't want to miss it.

Reel Nature by Gregg Mitman – published 1999 by Harvard University Press

In this book Gregg Mitman explores the history of nature films focusing on the conflict between the desire for scientific authenticity and the demand for audience-pleasing dramatisation. He discusses the driving forces behind the evolution of nature films over the decades, highlights good and bad nature film-makers, explores the relationship between scientific establishments and Hollywood, and analyses Disney's contributions to this genre and the huge success of natural history on TV. He finishes by concluding that while nature films help us to understand the natural world, the truth about our place in the web of life has been left on the cutting-room floor.

Celebrity and the Environment by Dan Brockington – published by Zed Books 2009

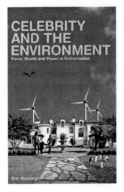

The battle to save the world is being joined by a powerful new group of warriors. Celebrities are lending their name to conservation causes, and conservation itself is growing its own stars to fight and speak for nature. In this timely and essential book, Dan Brockington argues that this alliance grows from the mutually supportive publicity celebrity and conservation causes provide for each other, and more fundamentally, that the flourishing of celebrity and charismatic conservation is part of an ever-closer intertwining of conservation and corporate capitalism. Celebrity promotions, the investments of rich executives, and the wealthy social networks of charismatic conservationists are producing more commodified and commercial conservation strategies; conservation becomes an ever more important means of generating profit. 'Celebrity and the Environment' provides vital critical analysis of this new phenomena and argues that, ironically, there may be a hidden cost to celebrity power to individual's relationships with the wild. The author argues that whilst wildlife television documentaries flourish, there is a significant decline in visits to national parks in many countries around the world and this is evidence that at a time when conservationists are calling for us to restore our relationships with the wild, many people are doing so simply by following the exploits of celebrity conservationists.

Contributors' Index

Many thanks to the following contributors to this book. Here you will find their contact details and a bit more about what they do. Note that the '+' on the telephone numbers requires the international access code which is usually 00, and numbers in brackets e.g. (0) would be omitted if dialling from abroad. Contributors are listed in alphabetical order of surname:

Professor Dennis Aig
Program Head, MFA in Science and Natural History Filmmaking
School of Film and Photography
Montana State University-Bozeman
227 Visual Communications Building, P.O. Box 173350
Bozeman, MT 59717-3350 USA
Telephone (Office): (+1) 406-994-6216   Mobile: (+1) 406-570-9505
Email: daig@montana.edu
Website: http://naturefilm.montana.edu

The Montana State University MFA in Science and Natural History Filmmaking trains aspiring filmmakers with scientific backgrounds to develop the creative, technical, and critical skills needed to create innovative work that will contribute to a better public understanding of science. The rigorous three-year program prepares students for careers in professional media production, government and NGO work, and academia.

Casey Anderson
Presenter/ EP 'Expedition Wild'
Email: casey@caseyanderson.tv
Website: www.caseyanderson.tv
Author of "The Story of Brutus"

Jonathan D. Andrews
Telephone: +1 (216) 789 2337
Email: Aliensound@mac.com

Alien Sound Inc. is a full service company that provides production sound mixers for wildlife or expedition documentaries. We are able to provide a full sound crew for a feature documentary or a crew of multiple sound mixers under the supervision of a sound supervisor for an adventure reality series, or a single mixer to go into the field alone and return with the sound you want and need.

Steve Backshall
Website: www.stevebackshall.com

Nick Baker
Email: info@dfmangement.tv
Website: www.nickbaker.tv

Rita Banerji
Dusty Foot Productions
C-9/9037 Vasant Kunj, New Delhi 110070 India
Telephone: +91 (11) 41081846 Mobile: +91 9810250260
Email: dustyfootindia@yahoo.com
Website: www.dustyfootindia.com

Rita Banerji heads Dusty Foot Productions, based in New Delhi, India. Established in 2002, Dusty Foot takes on projects on wildlife and environment panning from films, video documentation to education and outreach. Dusty Foot has an in-house team of technicians, and offers production and technical support for film projects. Currently Dusty Foot Projects are spread across the country from the Northeast of India, Western Ghats to Coastal India.

Janice Beatty
African Environments Ltd
PO Box 16080, Arusha, Tanzania
Telephone: +255 (0)733 508625
Email: janiceb@africanenvironments.com
Website: www.africanenvironments.com

African Environments' aim is to provide a responsible, reliable, environmentally friendly solution for film crews. With 20 years experience fixing in Tanzania on a wide variety of productions from blue-chip wildlife to a BBC comedy series we are a one-stop shop from permitting to 4x4 filming vehicles and camps. From our logistical base in Arusha we have organised many productions across the country and can also help in South Sudan and the DRC. We also outfit mountain climbs, vehicle and walking safaris.

Caroline Brett
Freelance Producer/Director
Shake the Tree Productions Ltd.
Hall Farm House, Suffield, Norfolk NR11 7EW, UK
Telephone: +44 (0)1263 768203
Email: carolinebrett@mac.com
Website: www.shakethetree.co.uk

Caroline Brett (BSC Hons Bristol University, Media Diploma UEA) is a highly

214

experienced and award-winning, freelance producer/director. She has written seven books on wildlife, had numerous articles published. She is experienced in operating video cameras, recording sound and taking stills. Her photographs are housed at the Specialist Stock Film Library. Caroline teaches filming, research and production, and writing for wildlife filmmakers on a one to one basis and through Wildeye courses.

Richard Brock
Executive Producer
Living Planet Productions & The Brock Initiative
Dumpers Cottage, Chew Magna, Bristol BS40 8SS, UK
Telephone: +44 (0)1275 333187 Mobile: +44 (0)7968 365816
Email: livingplanetproductions@gmail.com
Website: www.brockinitiative.org

I try to get stuff out there that will make a difference. There are now more ways of doing that than ever before. It can be in any format, anywhere, anyhow. I will provide free footage on wildlife and environmental matters from around the world. I am always interested in issues where "Filming with Attitude" might help the planet. Just let me know.

Dan Brockington
Email: dan.brockington@manchester.ac.uk

Dan Brockington is a Reader in Environment and Development at the University of Manchester who has undertaken research into diverse aspects of environmentalism and conservation since the mid-1990s. His books include *Fortress Conservation*, *Nature Unbound*, and *Celebrity and the Environment*. He is currently exploring the interactions between the celebrity industry and the NGO sector over the last 25 years.
 More details about his work are available at:
www.environmentalismandconservation.wordpress.com

Dean Burman
Telephone: +44 (0)1782 505 271 or +44 (0)7966 250 834
Email: dean.films@hotmail.co.uk
Website: www.waterwolf-produtions.co.uk

Dean Burman is a freelance natural history cameraman who films both topside and underwater. He has experience in filming in temperate, warm and tropical waters, and is capable of working solo or as part of a team. Dean has worked on and supplied footage for programmes including *Planet Earth*, *Countrylives* and *Deadly 60*.

Adrian Cale
Telephone: +44 (0)77 8920 5211
Email: acale@pupfishproductions.co.uk
Website: www.adriancale.co.uk

I am an accomplished Self-Shooting Producer / Director who has filmed, produced, directed, written and often presented natural history content for various broadcast and production partners. My combination of skill sets can compliment a number of crewing options and allow me to accommodate flexible and demanding budgets. I also develop my own independent film projects (as Pupfish Productions) which affords me a clear understanding of what it takes to carry a good programme idea through from concept to completion.

Richard Crosby
Films at 59
59 Cotham Hill, Clifton, Bristol,UK. BS6 6JR, UK
Telephone: +44 (0)117 9064300
Email: rjc@filmsat59.com
Website: www.filmsat59.com

Films at 59 are one of the major facilities for pre- and post-production in the UK, providing a one-stop-shop for production companies, being able to supply camera and audio equipment for the initial shoot right through the editing, offline and online processes, multimedia enabling such as DVD or Blue-ray authoring, Multi-format vision mastering, Hi-Definition and 3D with sophisticated multi-channel audio from mono through stereo to 5.1 and beyond with 7.1 and 9.1 formats possible and specialist super-surround for exhibitions and venues such as the Eden Project. We offer a crew diary service and have very experienced specialist staff in all areas.

Jenny Devitt
21 Sydling Road, Yeovil. Somerset, BA21 5LH, UK
Telephone: +44 (0)1935 410511 mobile/cell: +44 (0)7707 007099
Email: jenny.devitt@baobabproductions.co.uk
Website: www.baobabproductions.co.uk

Jenny has been a freelance documentary producer/writer/narrator since 1989 (several years with Partridge Films). She has written series and one-off wildlife documentaries for the BBC, Channel 4, Animal Planet, ABC Australia, ABC US and other international networks. Her company (Baobab Productions) is a small UK independent, offering broadcast and non-broadcast (corporate, educational, etc.) documentary and feature production, scriptwriting, editing and narration services. Special area of interest and expertise: natural history.

Henrik Ekman
SVT
SE-10510 Stockholm, Sweden
Telephone: +46 70 5438902
Email: henrik.ekman@svt.se

I work as a buyer of science and nature documentaries for the Swedish public broadcaster SVT. Along with this task I produce wildlife films and write books in the same genre. The past few years it has been a lot about wolves, resulting in two films and a book published in Sweden in 2010. Our acquisitions department mainly buys from the shelf, but occasionally we do pre-buys if the idea is good enough. Co-productions are rare.

Georgina Eyre
Head of Acquisitions
Off the Fence
Herengracht 105-107, 1015 BE Amsterdam, The Netherlands
Telephone: +31 20 5200 222
Website: www.offthefence.com

Off the Fence (OTF), is an independent television distribution company specialized in non-fiction content for the international marketplace. Since 1994 we've been creating and marketing high quality programming, focusing on integrity and innovation. OTF's comprehensive catalogue contains an impressive 4,500 hours of nature & wildlife, people, places & culture, travel & adventure, science & technology, history and lifestyle. And our expertise doesn't stop there. We also develop, finance, produce and co-produce international non-fiction programmes.

Alastair Fothergill
BBC Natural History Unit

Alastair Fothergill joined the BBC Natural History Unit in 1983. He has worked on a wide range of the department's programmes, including *The Trials of Life*, and *Life in the Freezer*, a series for BBC1 celebrating the wildlife of the Antarctic, presented by Sir David Attenborough. While still working on this series, he was appointed Head of the BBC Natural History Unit in November 1992, aged 32. In June 1998 he stood down as Head of the Unit to concentrate on his role as Series Producer of *The Blue Planet*. He was Series Producer for *Planet Earth*, the ultimate portrait of our planet, and Executive Producer on *Frozen Planet*, a natural history of the Polar Regions. In addition to his work with the BBC Natural History Unit, Alastair has his own production company and is presently directing two cinematic movies for Disney as part of their Disney Nature label.

Emma Fraser
Email: emma_lou_fraser@hotmail.com
IAWF profile at www.iawf.org.uk/profiles/member.asp?membersid=1211
Tigress Productions:
Website: www.tigressproductions.co.uk/

Tigress Productions Limited makes a wide range of adventure, science and wildlife documentaries, from the extraordinary series following climbers on Everest for Discovery: *Everest – Beyond the Limit*, to the curious anthropology series for Five: *Return of the Tribe*.

William Goodchild
Composer, Orchestrator, Conductor.
Studio 26, 42 Triangle West, Park Street, Bristol BS8 1ES, UK
Telephone: +44 (0)117 973 2297 Mobile: +44 (0)7814 234451
Email: mail@williamgoodchild.com
Website: www.williamgoodchild.com
Blog: http://williamgoodchild.blogspot.com

William Goodchild composes and produces music for film and television specialising in wildlife documentary. Projects for all the major broadcasters including BBC, Channel 4, Channel 5, PBS, National Geographic International and Animal Planet, including several award-winners. Full music production service for your film from initial ideas to delivered audio in stereo or 5.1 surround.

Steve Greenwood
Series Editor – *Natural World*
BBC Natural History Unit
Whiteladies Road, Bristol BS8 2LR, UK

Natural World is the BBC's strand of one-off wildlife documentaries and has been running for over twenty-eight years. The films we make are also regularly seen on Animal Planet, PBS and across the world on different channels. We are based at the Natural History Unit in Bristol.

Carl Hall
Parthenon Entertainment Limited
5 Station Approach, Chorleywood, Hertfordshire WD3 5PF, UK
Telephone: +44 (0)1923 286 886
Email: info@parthenonentertainment.com
Website: www.parthenonentertainment.com

Parthenon Entertainment Limited is a multi-media rights management company that develops, produces and distributes a diverse portfolio of high-quality factual and children's properties for the global marketplace. Founded in 2002 by Carl Hall, former managing director of HIT Wildlife, Parthenon is ranked amongst the top independent UK producers and distributors and has built a reputation for delivering high rating series and specials for clients around the world.

Neil Harraway
NHNZ Ltd
5 Melville Street, PO Box 474, Dunedin 9016, New Zealand
Telephone: +64 (0)3 4799799
Email: nharraway@nhnz.tv
Website: www.nhnz.tv

Neil Harraway is one of the original creative crew at NHNZ, which began life specialising in natural history some 30 years ago. In the last decade the company has evolved its expertise to include genres of science, adventure, history and people. NHNZ's successes range from acclaimed blue-chip series such as *Life Force* and *Wild Asia* and popular nature series such as *Built for the Kill* for Nat Geo Wild to cutting-edge science found in *China's Ghost Army* and gripping human stories in our series *I Survived* for A&E's Bio Channel. NHNZ is the largest producer of factual programming out of China, and was one of the first to embrace 3D documentary production.

Gail Jenkinson
Email: gailjenkinson1@me.com
Website: web.me.com/gailjenkinson1
Twitter: @gailiejenks

Gail is a freelance camera operator working in natural history and documentary film-making

Sandesh Kadur
Wildlife Filmmaker
Felis Creations – Bangalore, India
Gorgas Science Foundation – Brownsville, USA
Telephone: +1 202 657 4842 (Skype) +91 94480 59209 (India – mobile)
Email: kadur.sandesh@gmail.com
Website: www.felis.in

Felis Creations is a fully equipped documentary & photography service provider based in Bangalore, India. The company, founded in 2006, can help facilitate the production of documentaries on the Indian subcontinent, including Bhutan, Nepal and Sri Lanka. The company has on hire an array of HD equipment to suit any international production.

Mike Linley
Hairy Frog Productions
Telephone: +44 (0)7885 964790
Email: Hairyfrog@lineone.net
Website: www.hairy-frog.co.uk

Established in 2001, Hairy Frog Productions is an independent wildlife production and educational company. It has an extensive stills image library featuring a comprehensive selection of wildlife images and also a huge and varied range of flora, fauna, people and beautiful scenics from around the world. They have approximately 40,000 slides and 80,000 digital images and are growing daily. Hairy Frog also has a large sound library and wildlife stock footage digital video library. Rates are extremely competitive. They are fully equipped to film and edit in full HD. They specialise in providing stills, video clips and factual content for iPhone apps, Smart Boards and tables and touch screen digital displays.

Alan Miller
Editor/Writer/Director
Telephone: + 44 (0)1263 768203
Email: alanmiller@mac.com
Website:
http://web.me.com/alanmiller/Alan_Miller__Writer_Director_Editor/Welcome.html

Alan Miller has spent the last twenty-four years bringing the natural world to the global television and movie screen via a career encompassing editing, writing, directing and teaching. He's still not convinced by 3D though ...

Shinichi Murata
NHK (Japan Broadcasting Corporation)
2-2-1, Jin-nan, Shibuya, Tokyo, JAPAN 150-8001
Telephone:+81 3 3465 1111
Email: murata.s-gy@nhk.or.jp
Website: http://www.nhk.or.jp/hotspot/#/en/home

NHK is Japan's sole public broadcaster. Funded entirely by receiving fees from each Japanese household, it has a reputation for impartial, high-quality programming. Through its four nationwide TV channels, NHK reaches about 50 million households. Besides being a broadcaster, NHK produces a vast genre of high-quality programs from news, documentaries, talk shows, children and educational programs, music, entertainment, drama, and animation, all in HD. Most of NHK's programs are made available internationally through its affiliate NEP (NHK Enterprises, Inc.). www.nhk.or.jp/nhkworld

Professor Chris Palmer
Director of the Center for Wildlife Filmmaking
School of Communication, American University,
4400 Massachusetts Avenue, NW, Washington DC 20016-8017, USA
Telephone: +1 202-885-3408; cell +1 202-716-6160
Email: palmer@american.edu
Website: www.environmentalfilm.org

Chris Palmer is an environmental and wildlife film producer, speaker, author, and a professor who, over the past 30 years, has led the production of more than 300 hours of original programming for primetime television and the giant screen film industry. In 2004, he joined American University's full-time faculty as Distinguished Film Producer in Residence at the School of Communication. There he founded (and currently directs) the Center for Environmental Filmmaking. His book, *Shooting in the Wild: An Insider's Account of Making Movies in the Animal Kingdom*, was published in 2010 by Sierra Club Books and has been widely praised. He is also president of One World One Ocean, a campaign to save the oceans, and he serves on fourteen non-profit boards.

Louise Purnell
2 Heron Rd, Twickenham, Middlesex, TW1 1PG, UK
Telephone: 07766815974
Email: louise_purell@hotmail.com
Website: http://flavors.me/louise_purnell

Freelance camera assistant and film-maker specialising in documentary. My love of travel, and interest in wildlife, conservation and education, has led me to work on film projects across the world from Africa to the Arctic. Since 2003 I have worked for most major broadcasters and production companies including BBC, CH4, ITV, SKY, Endemol, Tiger Aspect and Ricochet.

Alex Rhodes
Telephone: +44 (0)1275 373382 Mobile: +44 (0)7554 575 949
Email: all@rhodesinternet.com

Alex is a young film-maker, photographer and naturalist based near Bristol, UK. He has aspirations to become a wildlife camera operator for a career and is making his mark in the industry from a young age. He has a breadth of knowledge about wildlife photography and is competent working on his own, in cramped spaces, at height or at night! He has spent many hours working in a hide and enjoys the challenge of a difficult shoot. He has two PADI qualifications, and is a trainee bird ringer for the BTO. He regularly shoots his own material and searches for work experience in assisting cameramen both in the field and studio.

Emma Rigney
Director of Development, Natural History
National Geographic Television
Email: erigney@ngs.org
Website: http://www.nationalgeographic.com/

Janet Rose
Executive Director/Festival Director
International Wildlife Film Festival
Montana CINE International Film Festival
International Media Center, 718 S. Higgins Avenue, c/o Roxy Theater,
Missoula, Montana 59801, USA
Telephone: (Cell): +1 406.880.0683 (Work): +1 406.728.9380
Email: jr1@wildlifefilms.org
Website: www.wildlifefilms.org

Janet Rose is the Executive Director/Festival Director of the International Wildlife Media Center & Film Festivals and has held this position for over 11 years. IWFF was the first wildlife film festival in the world and has evolved over the past decade to become a year round international media center hosting two annual film festivals, IWFF and now CINE. The organization is headquartered in Missoula, Montana. Janet is also a faculty affiliated in International Programs at The University of Montana. Prior to moving to Montana, Janet was a former television correspondent, specializing in investigative wildlife and environmental programs but also worked on news, policy and political issues within the broadcast field. She is a former producer and correspondent for a television news magazine, *Inside Report*. After leaving television, Janet was Head of Conservation Communications for the Wildlife Conservation Society based in NY. Janet's other personal passions are wildlife conservation, horse rescue and adoption, photography and her two wonderful daughters, Kara and Morissa.

Patrick Rouxel
Tawak Pictures
22 rue Davy, 75017 Paris, France
Email: patrickrouxel@hotmail.com

Freelance cameraman or director for environmental conservation films.

Mike Slee
Picture Projects
Summerlees House, Weston Green, Thames Ditton, Surrey KT7 0JZ, UK
Cell: +44 (0)7771 783 601
Website: www.mikeslee.co.uk

Mike Slee is a writer/film-maker, producer and executive producer specialising in factual features, documentary and science/natural history. Recent work has included 3D, large format, IMAX features and TV projects with complex CGI and reconstructed reality. Mike's projects have won a Wildscreen Panda, many international awards and Bafta nominations. Mike's Oscar shorlisted *BUGS!3D – A Rainforest Adventure* is the UK's highest-grossing natural history feature film.

Phil Streather
Stereo 3D Producer
Principal Large Format
The Old Vicarage, Leigh on Mendip, Somerset BA3 5QG, UK
Telephone: +44 (0)1373 813 301 Mobile: +44 (0)7771 783603
Email: phil@plf.cc
Skype: philstreather
Website: www.plf.cc

Phil Streather is the founder and CEO of Principal Large Format (PLF) specialising in Stereo 3D production and training. His 2003 IMAX film, *Bugs! 3D*, narrated by Judi Dench, has won many awards, including the prestigious Panda Award for Best Large Format Film at the Bristol Wildscreen Film Festival. In 2010 Phil produced *Carmen in 3D* from the Royal Opera House (directed by Julian Napier, and presented by RealD and Royal Opera House), shown in 1,500 cinemas worldwide Spring 2011, and has just delivered *Meerkats 3D*, produced by OSF in association with PLF, for National Geographic Channels/Sky 3D. Phil is currently (Summer 2011) in production on *Madama Butterfly 3D* from the Royal Opera House (directed by Julian Napier, presented by RealD and Royal Opera House).

Darryl Sweetland
Asian Wildlife Films Co., Ltd.
240/58 Moo 3, T. Khlong Kha Chen
Amphur Muang, Phichit 66000, Thailand
Telephone: + 66 (0)56 514963 (Home) + 66 (0)81 532 0303 (Mobile)
Email: darrylsweetland@yahoo.com
Website: www.asianwildlifefilms.com

Darryl Sweetland has spent the last 15 years exploring the wildlife and wild places of his adopted Thailand. He speaks, reads and writes Thai. Apart from filming his own projects, Darryl can make all necessary arrangements for visiting film crews, including advising on suitable locations and seasons to maximize the chances of a successful shoot.

Claire Thompson
Freelance Researcher
Telephone: +44 (0)7979 693975
Email: claire_t009@yahoo.co.uk

Experienced natural history researcher with a background in primate field research and conservation

Mat Thompson
UK-based Cameraman and Producer
Telephone: +44 (0)7967608239
Email: mdtmail@yahoo.co.uk
Twitter: @matthompson2010

Freelance cameraman & film-maker (experience includes: Panasonic Varicam, RED One/Epic, Canon DSLR, Sony EX, Olympus i-speed). I am a creative thinker who enjoys researching and developing stories. I also have the following additional skills: set construction for both topside and underwater sequences, experience working hands-on with animals and with animal husbandry. Also extensive CGI and post-production experience. I am now looking to extend my skills by taking on new projects and roles.

Gavin Thurston
Website: www.gavinthurston.com
Twitter: @gavinthurston

Gavin is available for camerawork, presenting, consultancy, training, corporates, talks, university-lectures.
Company website for equipment hire: www.movingpicturehire.com Moving Picture Hire Ltd can supply cable dollies, straight and curved lightweight track, motion control, time-lapse kits, LED lighting, video assist microwave links, remote hotheads, specialist lenses, custom grip design and build, and much more...

Laura Turner
Freelance Camera Operator and Editor at Ant Farm Films and The Wildlife Garden Project.
Telephone: +44 (0)7948 377224
Email: laura@antfarmfiilms.com
Website: www.antfarmfilms.com and www.wildlifegardenproject.com

I am an editor, camera operator and film-maker specialising in wildlife and conservation films. I set up *The Wildlife Garden Project*: a film and a website which aim to inspire people to make their gardens more wildlife friendly. Take a look at the website, or get in touch if you would like to discuss my services.

Sophie Vartan
NHU Africa
PO Box 12317, Mill Street, Gardens, Cape Town, 8010, South Africa
Telephone: +27 21 422 0154
Email: info@nhuafrica.com
Website: www.nhuafrica.com

Natural History Unit Africa (NHU Africa) commissions, co-produces and distributes wildlife and natural history documentaries and works with both international and local broadcasters. NHU Africa also runs Wild Talk Africa – an international wildlife film festival and conference – as well as the Wildlife Film Academy, a one-month course based in the heart of the South Africa bushveld. Another NHU Africa initiative is hosting the Wildlife Photographer of the Year exhibition for the Natural History Museum of London.

Ben Waddams
Ben Waddams Wildlife Art
Telephone: +44 (0)7793561912
Email: benwaddams@hotmail.com
Website: www.waddams.webs.com

Ben Waddams Wildlife Art provides artwork for individuals, companies, books and other publications. Fine art on a wildlife and sporting theme is produced for gallery exhibitions and exhibition shows and Ben's work in oils, acrylics and pen & ink is created for journalistic illustrations and sale through his website. Ben is happy to accept commissions for small natural history filming and writing projects as well as art assignments. He is also available for art safaris and may be contacted via phone or email.

Nikki.Waldron
Email: Nikki.Waldron@bbc.co.uk

I am a staff Assistant Producer at the BBC Natural History Unit with experience in a range of programming from children's to blue-chip and even live. I have been making wildlife documentaries for nine years and am a basic camera operator and editor as well as a producer/director.

Tom Walmsley
Director
Specialist Stock
Telephone: 01275 375520
Email: tom@specialiststock.com
Websites: www.SpecialistStock.com   www.SpecialistMediaTraining.com

Specialist Stock offers a number of services (www.SpecialistStock.com/services). As a comprehensive collection of photo and footage libraries we license material and multimedia Photostories to the global media industry. Through our Comprehensive Research Facility we search our global supplier network for any subject matter and sort out the licenses. Finally we give consultations and seminars to individuals and businesses who are 'Adopting a Video Workflow' by going through the options, technical details and business plan. Visit separate website: www.SpecialistMediaTraining.com.

John Watts
Director of Sales & Acquisitions
OCTAPIXX WORLDWIDE
200 Tiffield Road, Suite 101, Toronto, ON. CANADA. M1V 5J1
Telephone: (416) 449-9400 ext. 222
Email: jwatts@octapixx.com
Website: www.octapixx.com

Originally established in 1995, Octapixx Worldwide has grown into a *multi-dimensional* company. Octapixx successfully *sells* to and *professionally services* the key broadcasters, networks, distributors and multimedia companies around the world. Octapixx is located in Toronto, Canada, well recognized by the industry as an economically stable centre for production and investment with serious growth potential. Octapixx Worldwide currently represents over 75 producers from around the globe and Octapixx's library now hosts over 1100 hours of top quality television programming.

Sue Western
Telephone: +44 (0)117 9735473 or +44 (0)7870 977762
Email: sue.western@blueyonder.co.uk

When it's difficult to see the wood for the trees, I'm the **fresh pair of eyes** that provides clarity, and nudges a project back on track. I can supply story advice from the outset, act as a mid-production sounding-board, offer structural guidance in the cutting room, write or script edit the final commentary, or even provide a full remedial service for films in distress. My aim, always, is to add value – to unlock the full potential of a story and make a film the *best* it can be.

Cody Westheimer
New West Studios, Inc.
Email: cody@codywestheimer.com
Website: www.codywestheimer.com

Led by composer couple Cody Westheimer and Julia Newmann, New West Studios, Inc is a full service music production and recording facility focusing on film and television. Located in West Los Angeles, their facility is watched by a coastal redwood that towers over the property. Rounded out by a koi pond, their state of the art setup can draw inspiration to the largest Hollywood project or to the smallest independent film.

Madelaine Westwood
Nutshell Productions Ltd
3 Westfield Cottages, Medmenham, Marlow, Bucks SL7 2HQ, UK.
Telephone: +44 (0)1491 575 017\ 07770 577 549
Website: www.nutshellproductions.co.uk

Nutshell Productions crosses the spectrum of film production, producing films for international broadcasters through to issue-films created in association with local communities. Engaging an audience in such a way that they are able to contribute in some way to the information, issues, challenges that they have viewed is top priority for our productions. In this spirit we offer productions, co-productions, distribution, training, media advice and support to any NGO or conservation organisation whilst producing high quality series and one-offs for international distribution.

Mark Wild
artists in motion
Telephone : +44(0) 7973 754 759
Email: mark@artistsim.com
Website: www.artistsim.com

Mark Wild is Joint Managing Director and handles creative and production aspects of artists in motion. Mark is a multi-award winning producer and director of global television programmes with twenty years of experience in the UK film and television industry. Recently Mark served as Director of International Development in the London office of National Geographic Television and prior to this as Head of Production and Development for Animal Planet International with the Discovery Channel. To date, he has garnered 114 awards for the programmes and films he has helped to develop and create including *Ocean Voyagers* (Japanese Film Festival 2009); *Meerkat Manor* (Wildscreen 2008); and *Crime Scene Wild* (Jackson Hole 2007).

Kim Wolhuter
Mavela Media,
Postnet Suite 256, Private Bag X11326, Nelspruit, South Africa 1200
Telephone: Cell +27 83 455 7970
Email: wildhoot@mweb.co.za

I work as a cameraman and producer, mainly producing high-end natural history films. All my work is carried out in Africa, mainly southern Africa, and at the moment I'm based on Malilangwe Reserve, Zimbabwe, where I have exclusive filming rights. I also specialise in shooting at night.

Jackson Xu
Images Biodiversity Expedition Ins.
Youlehui C-3001, WangJingYuan 603, Chaoyang district, Beijing,
China 100102
Telephone: +86-10-64777035
Email: xujian@IBEwildlife.com or jacksonxuphoto@gmail.com

Images Biodiversity Expedition Ins. (IBE) was founded in 2008 in Beijing. The objective of the studio is recording, spreading and protecting the biodiversity of China, as it is quickly disappearing. IBE consists of a group of Chinese active young wildlife photographers, wildlife film-makers, eco-designers and conservationists. They have done sixteen expeditions in nine biodiversity key areas of China from 2008 to June 2011. The results were biodiversity picture albums, documentaries, expedition reports and conservation recommendation reports.

Joe Yaggi
Jungle Run Productions
Telephone: +62361979109 Mobile: +628123813887
Email: joe@jungle-run.com
Skype: : joe2jungle

Website: www.jungle-run.com

Jungle Run is a full service production house strategically based on the island Bali in Indonesia. We have full HD crews, camera kits and post-production facilities for projects from concept to completion. We offer production and location management services and film permit facilitation for visiting producers and broadcasters. Our stock footage library carries HD video and digital stills from across the archipelago ranging from pristine wilderness and wildlife to concrete jungles. For a great production experience in an amazing country, please give us a call.

Xi Zhinong
Wild China Film
No. 137 Xizhimenwai Dajie, Beijing, China 100044
Telephone/Fax: +86 10 8836 7109
Email: xizhinong@wildchina.cn
Website: www.wildchina.cn

Wild China Film is an independent, professional organization, dedicated to promoting conservation through images. It specializes in documenting China's wildlife, nature and environment, using both still and moving images, and it is committed to mobilizing the power of images to promote public participation in conservation. Wild China Film was founded in 2002 by China's best known wildlife photographer and conservationist, Xi Zhinong.

Since the late 1990s **Wildlife-film.com** has been the leading source of information for the wildlife film-making industry worldwide. For over twelve years the site has been Google's number one ranking site for 'wildlife film' and related searches. The website is viewed in over 175 countries.

The newsletter, **Wildlife Film News**, is read every month by thousands of people involved in wildlife film-making - from broadcasters and producers to freelancers and newcomers - we encourage readers to submit their news.

Wildlife-film.com also serves as an online resource for industry professionals and services. Find producers, editors, presenters and more in the **Freelancer** section, and find out about festivals, training and conservation in **Organisations**. We encourage amateur and professional freelancers to join our network and welcome all wildlife-film related organisations to join our team.

www.wildlife-film.com